L.A. Landmarks

LOST AND ALMOST LOST

Cindy Olnick

PHOTO FRIENDS
of the LOS ANGELES PUBLIC LIBRARY
PUBLICATIONS

Contents

ALMOST LOST

Introduction

What's your favorite Los Angeles landmark? Does it still stand, or is it just a memory?

Angelenos have been demolishing landmarks as long as we've been building them. Nearly every square inch of the city used to be something else, and many places that rose on the ashes of landmarks have gained their own significance over time.

Most of what we typically consider landmarks are beautiful works of architecture, but they're also much more. Landmarks distinguish and anchor communities. They're tangible history, offering an experience that words or images never could. They connect us with our past and each other. They educate and inspire. They reflect our values as a society. Some landmarks are icons; others are neighborhood gems. Some aren't even pretty, but they play key roles in conveying our culture.

It's hard to hold on to our landmarks in a city like Los Angeles, which has reinvention in its DNA. The freedom and innovation that fostered L.A.'s unique architectural legacy now threaten its survival—particularly in a place with relentless development pressure and concentrated power over land-use decisions.

Stylistic trends also play a role. Downtown's Richfield Building was an Art Deco masterpiece demolished in 1968, when many considered the style passé. Landmarks are particularly vulnerable at around age forty—like the Richfield—and their style has reached its nadir. By the time the pendulum of popular taste swings back in their direction, it's too late.

The good news is, a lot of people care about historic places in Los Angeles, and they work tirelessly to preserve them. We all play a role, from leading preservation efforts, to contacting elected officials when an important place is threatened, to sharing our love of landmarks with our friends.

Some people consider "historic Los Angeles" an oxymoron. Yes, L.A. is a relatively young city; our landmarks need a chance to grow old. If we can keep them standing long enough—occupied and relevant—just imagine the legacy Los Angeles can have centuries from now.

This book highlights just a few of the many landmarks in and near Los Angeles that fell to the wrecking ball or narrowly escaped. There's much more to each of these stories, and there are many more stories like them.

Some of the stories cross paths in unexpected ways. The original home of the Atomic Café was razed to make way for Parker Center, now itself slated for demolition. Bart Lytton, who tore down the Garden of Allah to build a bank (now itself a landmark and facing demolition), tried to preserve the Dodge House as part of a housing development. One place is both lost *and* almost lost: Terminal Island, which lost its Japanese fishing village to bigotry in World War II but retains the last remnants of its rich maritime and commercial history.

I hope these images illustrate not just pretty buildings, but the integral role of historic places in our lives. Preservation is really about people, and it takes people to save what's left of our cultural heritage.

—CINDY OLNICK
Board Member, Photo Friends
Former Director of Communications, Los Angeles Conservancy

LO

ST

Terminal Island Fishing Village

(c. 1900 – 1942)

PORT OF LOS ANGELES, SAN PEDRO

At the turn of the twentieth century, a dozen Japanese fishermen settled on Terminal Island at the Port of Los Angeles. At around the same time, a cannery on the island perfected a method for canning tuna that made it marketable as an affordable substitute for chicken. Within a decade, Los Angeles had launched a worldwide industry that made canned tuna a household staple. The Japanese settlers proved to be master commercial fishermen, and they taught Americans and other immigrants.

By the 1940s, the island housed a thriving community of nearly 3,000 Japanese and Japanese American residents. It was essentially a company town, with husbands fishing and wives canning. The neighborhood had Buddhist temples, a Shinto shrine, a Baptist church, a bank, a school, a judo hall, and a pool hall. Residents kept their rich traditions alive, creating a hybrid culture of their homeland and their new home.

Located next to a U.S. Navy facility, these residents were also the first Japanese Americans to be forcibly removed from their homes after the bombing of Pearl Harbor in December 1941. After the evacuation in February 1942, the Navy demolished everything in the village except a few commercial buildings.

Carp windsocks float above homes as part of *Tango no Sekku*, the annual Boys' Festival (now Children's Day). The poles hold one fish for each boy in the family, sized according to age. (1925, Security Pacific National Bank Collection)

This Shinto shrine was part of Terminal Island's vibrant Japanese American community. It was destroyed, along with the rest of the village, after the residents were sent to internment camps in World War II. Only a few commercial buildings remain. (Circa 1920, Security Pacific National Bank Collection)

Residents enjoy a kid-powered merry-go-round, part of the celebration of both the Boys' Festival and May Day. (Circa 1925, Security Pacific National Bank Collection)

The Garden of Allah Hotel and Villas spanned three and a-half acres on the western edge of Hollywood. In this photo, Sunset Boulevard is in the foreground and Havenhurst Drive is on the right. (Undated, Security Pacific National Bank Collection)

Garden of Allah

(1927 – 1959)

8152 SUNSET BLVD., HOLLYWOOD

The Garden of Allah is one of L.A.'s most romanticized lost landmarks. Spanning three and a-half acres at Sunset and Crescent Heights Boulevards, the hotel grew out of the estate of Russian-born actress Alla Nazimova, who held popular salons for fellow ex-patriots and intellectuals.

Expanded into a hotel in 1927, the bungalows at the Garden of Allah hosted actors, writers, musicians—a roster of A-listers that became a close-knit community of creative souls. Residents included Orson Welles, Dorothy Parker, and Artie Shaw, to name just a few. The hotel was an instant hit but ruined Nazimova financially; she ended up living in one of the villas.

The Garden's popularity declined over the fifties, and in 1959 financier and arts patron Bart Lytton bought the property. He razed the Garden of Allah and replaced it with new headquarters for the Lytton Savings and Loan Association, which included an arts center for the public. The 1960 building designed by Kurt Meyer has itself become significant and is a designated local landmark. As of 2017, it is also threatened with demolition for a new development designed by Frank Gehry.

The Garden of Allah Hotel the year it opened. It was surrounded by twenty-five bungalows and hosted a who's who of Hollywood for decades. (1927, Security Pacific National Bank Collection)

Looking east down Sunset Boulevard, the building with the folded-plate roof is the former Lytton Savings building, which replaced the Garden of Allah. This 1960 building by Kurt Meyer has gained significance in its own right and is now a local landmark. It is also threatened with demolition as of 2017. (1979, Roy Hankey Collection)

Opposite: The Garden of Allah was razed in 1959 and replaced with new headquarters for the Lytton Savings and Loan Association. The Lytton Center of the Visual Arts, one of the earliest corporate arts programs, operated in the building until 1969. The original caption for this photo reads, "Visitors eye shadow boxes at Lytton Center." The article partially reads, "For the uninitiated, phenakistoscoping is what folks used to do before drive-in movies. It involves looking through a little slit in a spinning wheel and enjoying the illusion that a clown inside is jumping up and down..." (1963, George Brich/Valley Times Collection)

NBC Radio City Hollywood

(1938 – 1964)

1500 VINE ST., HOLLYWOOD

NBC Radio City Hollywood exemplified the heyday of Hollywood as a broadcasting hub. Renowned architect John C. Austin designed the sprawling Streamline Moderne complex, which contained eight studios and three office buildings. It opened in 1938 at the northeast corner of Sunset and Vine, a site steeped in Hollywood history. It was the former site of the Famous Players-Lasky Studios (which became Paramount Pictures) and the Lasky-DeMille Barn (see page 139).

The main lobby rose three stories and embodied the power of radio, from a soaring mural by Edward Turnbull (who also painted the lobby ceiling of the Chrysler Building) to zigzag sound waves coursing through the terrazzo floor.

As television broadcasting emerged full force, NBC outgrew the studios and built new ones in Burbank. The entire site was demolished in 1964 and replaced with a Home Savings and Loan (now Chase) branch designed by Millard Sheets. Now a significant landmark in its own right, the building features mosaic murals depicting early Hollywood stars in their signature roles, an homage to the site's origins.

The Streamline Moderne NBC Radio City Hollywood dominated the corner of Sunset and Vine. (1958, Security Pacific National Bank Collection)

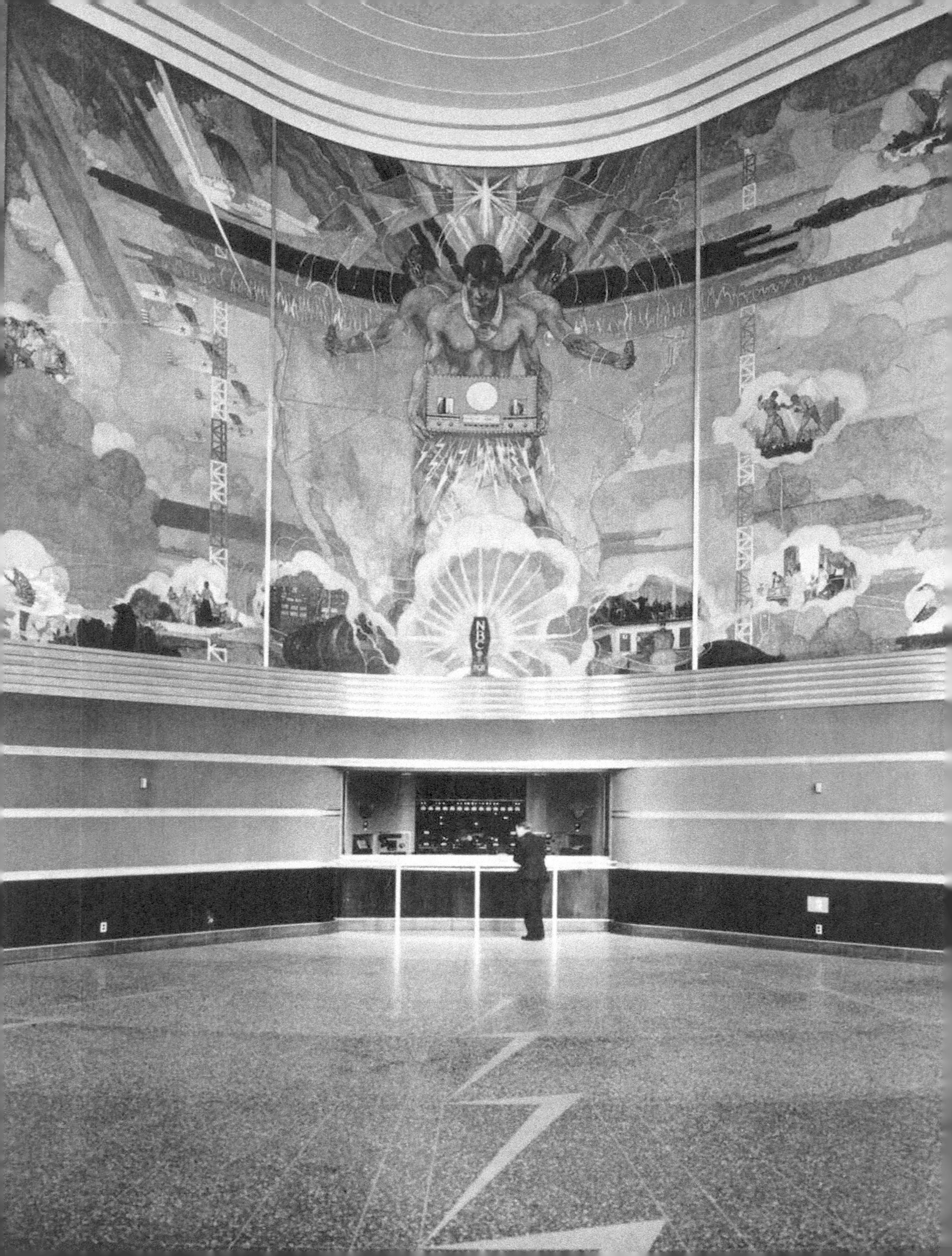
NBC

Sunset Boulevard looking west from Vine Street, with the main entrance to the NBC complex on the right. (Undated, Security Pacific National Bank Collection)

Opposite: **The towering lobby featured a massive mural by Edward Turnbull depicting the power of radio. (1938, Security Pacific National Bank Collection)**

A sunset view of the Sunset façade.
(1938, Security Pacific National Bank Collection)

Legendary singer Nat King Cole (seated) at the studios with bassist Joe Comfort (left) and singer Dick Haymes (leaning over Cole's shoulder). (Circa 1949, Shades of L.A.: African American Community)

Demolition of the complex, which was replaced by a Millard Sheets-designed branch of Home Savings and Loan, now itself a landmark. (1964, Robert R. Jensen/ Security Pacific National Bank Collection)

Richfield Building

(1928 – 1968)
555 S. FLOWER ST., DOWNTOWN

The Richfield Building was an icon of Art Deco architecture. Built in 1928 and designed by Stiles O. Clements of Morgan, Walls, and Clements, the headquarters of the Richfield Oil Company was clad in black and gold terra cotta, symbolizing to many the "black gold" of Richfield's business.

The twelve-story building rose in a series of setbacks, culminating in a 130-foot tower with RICHFIELD spelled out in neon. The façade featured sculpted figures by Haig Patigian, including forty winged sentries—each ten feet tall and weighing more than a ton—perched along the roofline.

Crowning the main entrance were more stylized human figures holding trains, planes, and other symbols of motive power. The building's interior was equally spectacular, filled with black-and-green marble and bronze fixtures including highly ornamented elevator doors.

It's hard to believe today, but in the late 1960s, many considered the Art Deco style passé. Richfield had merged with Atlantic, creating the Atlantic Richfield Company, or ARCO. ARCO demolished the Richfield Building in 1968-69. Its replacement, twin towers of smooth granite flanking a public plaza, is now considered significant in its own right as a fine example of the Corporate International Style. Two of the Richfield's elevator doors stand as sculptural elements in the plaza.

The Richfield Building a week before its demolition. (1968, Security Pacific National Bank Collection)

Opposite: **The shining beacon of the Richfield Building at night, looking north on Flower Street from Wilshire Boulevard. (1966, Herald Examiner Collection)**

The spectacular entrance of the Richfield Building, crowned by sculpted figures holding symbols of motive power. (1963, William Reagh Collection)

Opposite: **Some of the forty winged sentries along the roofline, each standing ten feet tall and weighing more than a ton. (Undated, Security Pacific National Bank Collection)**

The stylish chevron design in the sidewalk in front of the Richfield Building offers a mere hint at the beauty inside. (Circa 1937, Herman J. Schultheis Collection)

Opposite: The demolition of the Richfield Building. (1969, Michael Haering/Herald Examiner Collection)

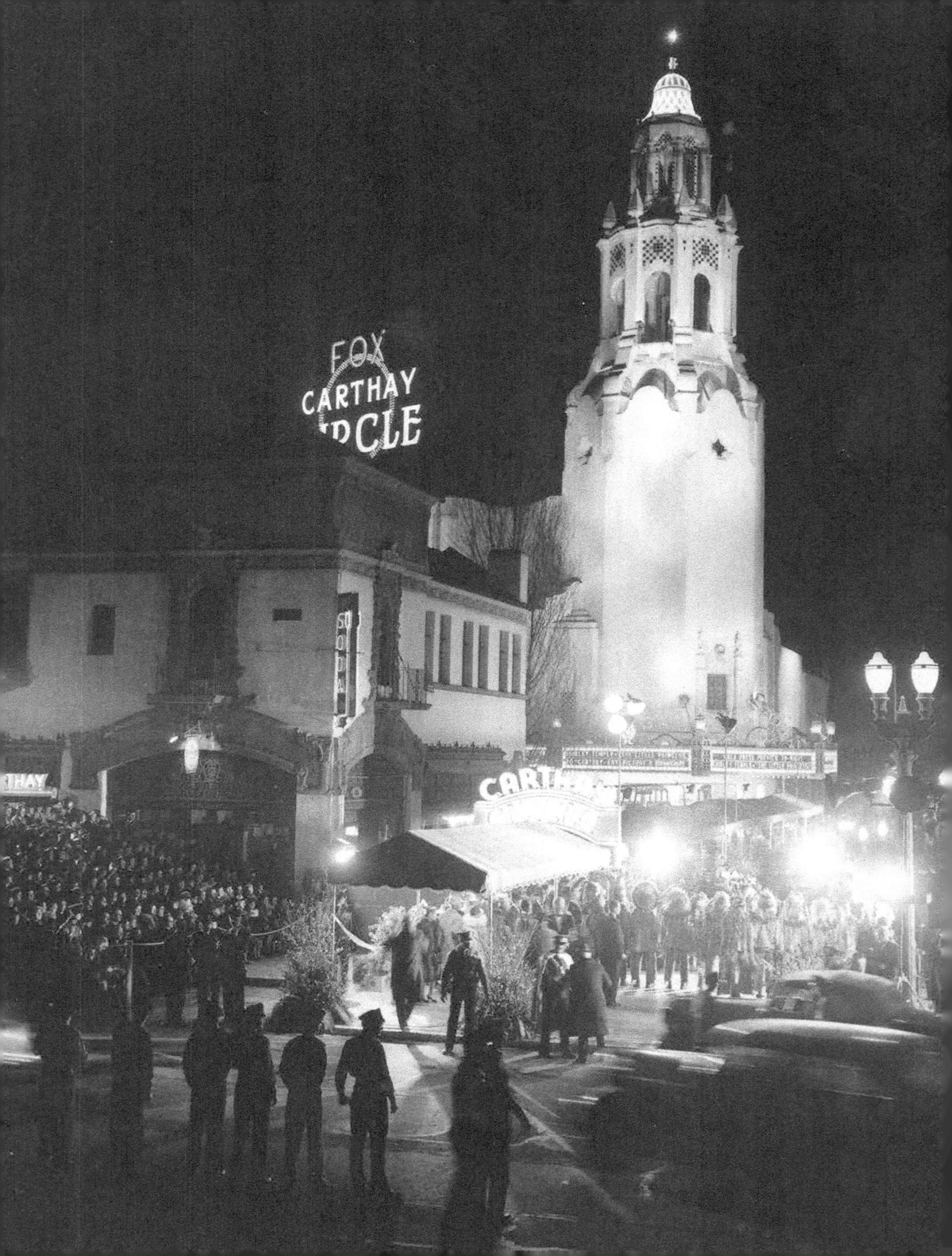
FOX
CARTHAY
SODA

Carthay Circle Theatre

(1926 – 1969)

6316 SAN VICENTE BLVD., CARTHAY CIRCLE

Designed by Dwight Gibbs, the Carthay Circle Theatre opened in 1926 with Cecil B. DeMille's *The Volga Boatman*. Despite its then-remote location at Wilshire Boulevard and what is now San Vicente Boulevard, the theatre became a major site for Hollywood premieres.

The Spanish Colonial Revival-style theatre was envisioned as a tribute to the founders and pioneers of California. It evoked the state's mission heritage, including an illuminated Spanish-style tower and murals, paintings, and artifacts depicting early California history. The theatre became known as "The Showplace of the Golden West."

Fox West-Coast Theatres took over the Carthay Circle in 1929. Premieres at the theatre evolved into major Hollywood sensations, with hundreds of fans waiting for a glimpse of the stars. When producer Mike Todd screened *Around the World in 80 Days* there in 1956, some of the theatre interior was destroyed to make room for his massive TODD-AO screen.

Like most other single-screen theatres, the Carthay Circle Theatre suffered tough competition from suburban multiplexes in the sixties. It was demolished in 1969 and replaced with an office building.

The Carthay Circle Theatre glows for the Gala Press Preview of *The Little Princess*, starring Shirley Temple. (1939, Herald Examiner Collection)

The original caption dated July 18, 1944 reads, "Shirley Temple, now a charming young lady instead of the tiny tot who used to be featured in Carthay Circle premieres, is shown arriving at the theater, accompanied by her mother and father, Mr. and Mrs. George Temple, and her escort for the gala evening, Pvt. Andy Hatchkiss, of the U.S. Army, right." (1944, Herald Examiner Collection)

Opposite: The original proscenium of the Carthay Circle Theatre, with its asbestos fire curtain. The proscenium was altered in 1956 to accommodate producer Mike Todd's 70mm TODD-AO screen. (1926, Security Pacific National Bank Collection)

Daytime view of the Carthay Circle Theatre,
then operated by Fox West Coast Theatres.
(1947, Security Pacific National Bank Collection)

The Salt Box and the Castle

(1880s – 1969)

339 AND 325 S. BUNKER HILL AVE., DOWNTOWN

Built in the 1880s, these two homes stood doors from each other on Bunker Hill. The modest Salt Box was nicknamed for its saltbox style; the twenty-room Castle, for its opulence. Both homes saw the transition of Bunker Hill from a tony enclave into a working-class neighborhood as Los Angeles expanded from the city center.

Despite its vibrancy, by the mid-twentieth century Bunker Hill was labeled as "blighted" by the City, making it a prime target for the "urban renewal" taking place across the U.S. As the Community Redevelopment Agency proceeded with the wholesale demolition of Bunker Hill, concerned citizens fought to preserve what they could. The Salt Box was designated as a Historic-Cultural Monument on the Cultural Heritage Board's first day of business in August 1962. The Castle's designation came two years later.

In March 1969, both homes were moved to the fledgling Heritage Square Museum in Montecito Heights. As community members raised funds for restoration, both homes were destroyed in an arson fire that October. Music fans seeking a glimpse of the Salt Box can find it on the cover of Taj Mahal's 1968 debut album.

The Salt Box in its original location at 339 S. Bunker Hill Ave. Looming behind it is the recently completed Union Bank Building, a harbinger of the new Bunker Hill. (1967, Security Pacific National Bank Collection)

Months after reaching their new home at Heritage Square, the Castle and the Salt Box succumb to a fire set by vandals on October 9, 1969. (1969, Herald Examiner Collection)

HERITAGE SQUARE

THESE TWO BUILDINGS "THE CASTLE" AND THE
SALT BOX WERE BROUGHT HERE FROM THEIR SITE
ON BUNKER HILL TO SERVE AS A LIVING REMINDER OF
THE ONCE ELEGANT VICTORIAN ERA IN LOS ANGELES.
THE CULTURAL HERITAGE BOARD NEEDS FUNDS TO
RESTORE THEM TO THEIR ORIGINAL BEAUTY FOR THE
ENJOYMENT OF YOU AND YOUR CHILDREN.

DONATIONS ACCEPTED BY
Municipal Art Patrons · Heritage Square
ROOM 1500 CITY HALL
LOS ANGELES - 90012

The remains of the Salt Box the morning after the fire. (1969, Herald Examiner Collection)

Dodge House

(1916 – 1970)
950 Kings Rd., West Hollywood

Built in 1916, the Walter L. Dodge House was considered by many as the first modernist residence in the West, as well as one of the most significant American homes of the twentieth century. Architect Irving Gill re-envisioned the Southern California home with new materials, techniques, and design concepts. He treated architecture and landscape as one, framing views, using shadows as ornament, and tinting the concrete to best reflect changing light patterns. He made the interior both beautiful, with rich mahogany paneling; and highly functional, with technical innovations for ease of maintenance. The home had what writer Jeffrey Head called "a stunningly beautiful sense of simplicity."

In 1939, the City of Los Angeles acquired the site through eminent domain for a high school. When those plans didn't materialize, it was used by the Frank Wiggins Trade School, now Los Angeles Trade-Technical College. In the early 1960s, the Board of Education declared the house "surplus" and slated it for demolition.

Renowned architectural historian and critic Esther McCoy led a campaign to prevent demolition of the Dodge House, which included a wonderful short film now available on YouTube. Financier Bart Lytton, who razed the Garden of Allah, bought the Dodge House and tried unsuccessfully to preserve it as part of a housing development.

The entire property was demolished, unannounced, in February 1970. From all accounts, the house did not go quietly, the eight-inch-thick concrete walls resisting the wrecking ball until they could no longer.

The entrance to the Dodge House property, which spanned several acres in the heart of West Hollywood. Imagine how striking it would have been in 1916, entirely unlike anything else at the time. (Undated, Security Pacific National Bank Collection)

A young woman decorates a cake in the kitchen of the Dodge House. After being acquired by the Los Angeles Board of Education in 1939, the house was used for "household service training" for the Frank Wiggins Trade School, now Los Angeles Trade-Technical College. (Undated, Los Angeles Trade-Tech Collection)

The Dodge House site after demolition, which destroyed everything, even longstanding trees. The property now contains condos. (1970, Guy Goodenow/ Herald Examiner Collection)

Von Sternberg House

(1935 – 1971)
10000 Tampa Ave., Northridge

In 1935, master architect Richard Neutra designed a home for director Josef von Sternberg, best known for his work with Marlene Dietrich. The home was a retreat twenty miles from Hollywood in the then-rural San Fernando Valley.

It was a masterpiece of aluminum and glass, with a large curved wall surrounding the front patio, a moat, and a rooftop reflecting pool. The interior included a double-height living room with a gallery for the owner's fine art. "That house was probably the most architecturally significant building ever in the Valley," renowned architectural historian Robert Winter told the *Los Angeles Times* in 1999.

Von Sternberg sold the residence in 1943, having tired of the remote location and the use of his home as a mock target by World War II pilots. Author Ayn Rand owned the house for several years and wrote much of *Atlas Shrugged* there. The next-door neighbor bought the home in 1963 and had it razed in 1971, apparently due to fear of "hippies" on the property (this was just a couple of years after the Manson murders). Fifteen-year-old neighbor Andy Moore captured some of the demolition on film, which is now on YouTube. The site later became a housing development.

**The rural retreat Richard Neutra designed for director Josef von Sternberg.
(1939, Burton O. Burt/Works Progress Administration Collection)**

Imagine this house in the 1930s, in the middle of orange groves. (1939, Burton O. Burt/Works Progress Administration Collection)

Behind the wall at the von Sternberg House, which featured a shallow moat and rooftop reflecting pool. (Circa 1936-38, Luckhaus Studio/Ralph Morris Collection)

Coulter's
(1938 – 1980)
5600 WILSHIRE BLVD., MIRACLE MILE

Coulter's on Wilshire Boulevard was one of the city's greatest examples of Streamline Moderne architecture. It was designed by Stiles O. Clements, a leader in the Art Deco and Streamline Moderne movements. Clements mastered a range of styles and designed many Los Angeles gems, including the Richfield Building (lost) and Wiltern Theatre (almost lost).

The sleek building featured rounded corners of white concrete, horizontal bands of glass instead of traditional windows, and a panel of glass blocks rising seventy-two feet above the Wilshire entrance.

Its opening also marked a milestone for the Miracle Mile, which was succeeding downtown as L.A.'s major shopping destination. Rather than opening a branch on Wilshire like other department stores, Coulter Dry Goods left downtown completely for the Miracle Mile.

The building changed hands in the 1960s, when The Broadway department store moved in. The owner demolished it in 1980, citing plans for a mixed-use development on the site. The property wasn't redeveloped until 2007. For twenty-eight years, the site was a massive pit oozing with tar and oil. Now it houses a massive mixed-use complex.

Stiles O. Clements designed this 1938 Streamline Moderne gem as the new Miracle Mile flagship for Coulter Dry Goods. It was one of the best examples of the style in Los Angeles. (Circa 1939, Works Progress Administration Collection)

The ladies' undergarment department at Coulter's, back when shopping was swank, even for regular people. (Undated, Security Pacific National Bank Collection)

Opposite: Coulter's was a key element of the Miracle Mile streetscape. (Undated, Security Pacific National Bank Collection)

The Broadway department store occupied the building from the 1960s until its demolition in 1980. (1978, Anne Laskey/Marlene Laskey/Wilshire Boulevard Collection)

After the building's demolition in 1980, the site stood vacant for nearly 30 years. Locals referred to it as The Pit, seen here in the foreground with the California Federal Savings & Loan building designed by Charles Luckman Associates. (Circa 2000, Robert Pacheco/Los Angeles Neighborhoods Collection)

Tiny Naylor's

(1949 – 1984)
7101 Sunset Blvd., Hollywood

W. W. "Tiny" Naylor (six-foot-four, 320 pounds) opened his first
Southern California restaurant at the northwest corner of Sunset
Boulevard and La Brea Avenue. The site previously housed a 1930s
McDonnell's drive-in.

Noted architect Douglas Honnold designed the modern marvel with
engineer Rich Bradshaw in 1949. Its gravity-defying canopies, sparkling
chrome and stainless
steel, and walls of
glass exemplified the
exuberant postwar
Googie style and
embodied L.A.'s car
culture.

Tiny Naylor's
survived for decades as

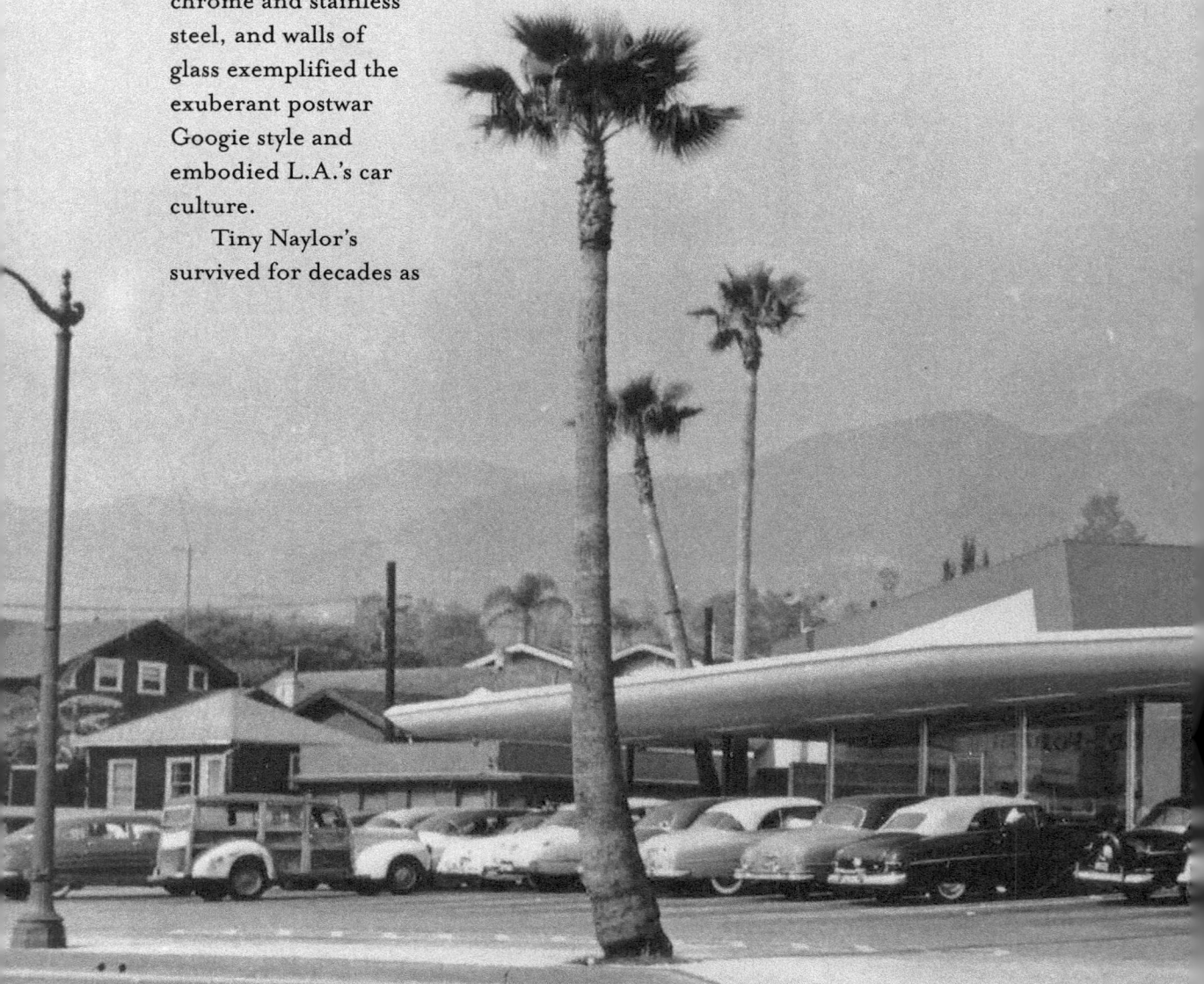

one of the last drive-in restaurants in Southern California. It closed in March 1984, slated for replacement with a new commercial building. The developers offered to donate the building to the Los Angeles Conservancy if they could find a new location for it. The Conservancy and the Friends of Tiny Naylor's rallied to save it and find a new location, to no avail. It was demolished that June.

The loss of Tiny Naylor's, and of the Ships Westwood coffee shop that same year, led to the formation of the Los Angeles Conservancy's volunteer Fifties Task Force, now the Modern Committee. Known as ModCom, the committee pioneered the preservation of postwar landmarks long before the renaissance of Mid-Century Modernism.

Tiny Naylor's in its heyday. Designed by Douglas Honnold in 1949, the drive-in embodied L.A.'s car culture and postwar optimism. It originally had a green-and-yellow color scheme. (Circa 1950s, Security Pacific National Bank Collection)

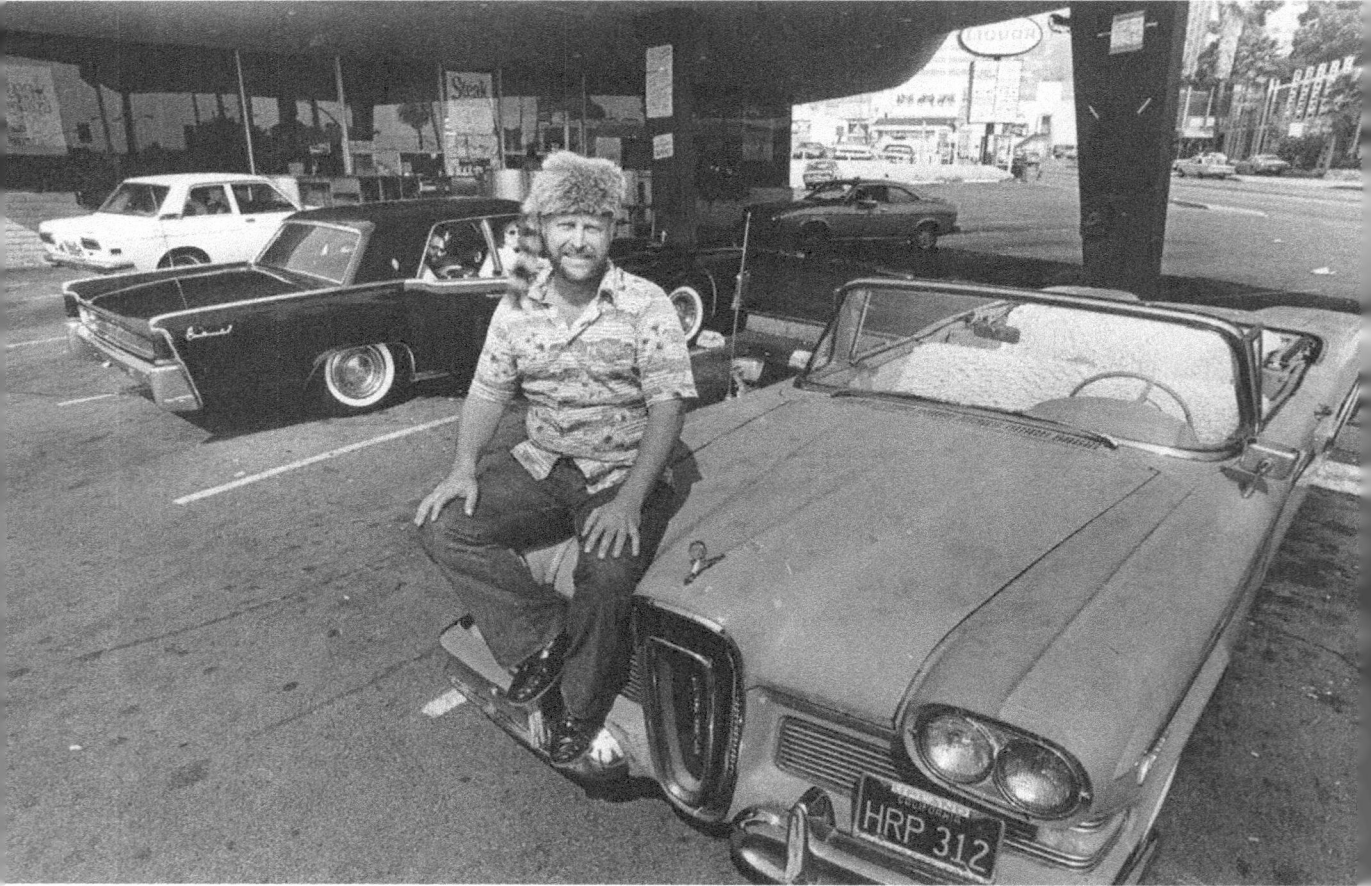

John Mouch of the Los Angeles Conservancy atop his Edsel outside Tiny Naylor's. The Conservancy featured the drive-in on its 1981 tour, "Cruisin' L.A.," which explored how the automobile shaped L.A.'s environment. (1981, Herald Examiner Collection)

The pop group the Bangles across the street from Tiny Naylor's. (1982, Gary Leonard/Herald Examiner Collection)

Brown Derby

(1936 - 1985)
3377 WILSHIRE BLVD., WILSHIRE CENTER

The first Brown Derby restaurant, and the only one in the shape of a hat, was built in 1926. Movie producer Herbert Somborn (Gloria Swanson's second husband) opened the restaurant with screenwriter Wilson Mizner and theatre impresario Sid Grauman, with Jack Warner reportedly a silent partner. Somborn wanted to provide his friends—the Hollywood A-list—with a place to enjoy great food in relative privacy.

The restaurant was built at 3427 Wilshire Boulevard, across the street from the Ambassador Hotel. In 1936, it moved half a block east to 3377 Wilshire, at the corner of Alexandria Avenue. The hat-shaped dome was rebuilt and a dining patio added.

The Wilshire Brown Derby remained a tourist destination long after the stars stopped coming. The restaurant closed suddenly in September 1980, and scaffolding rose around the dome. Concerned citizens sprang into action, picketing at the site to block demolition. Ultimately, the owner's children donated the dome to Hollywood Heritage and the Los Angeles Conservancy.

In 1985, the dome was incorporated into a strip mall on the site called the Brown Derby Plaza. It remains there today. While the dome technically still exists, its undignified treatment renders the Brown Derby a loss in this author's book.

The Wilshire Brown Derby was one of several locations in the restaurant chain, and the only one in the shape of a hat. (Circa 1930s, Security Pacific National Bank Collection)

Picketers protest in front of the Brown Derby after it closed suddenly in September 1980. A bulldozer arrived immediately after it closed, but citizens were able to stop the demolition. (1980, Mike Mullen/Herald Examiner Collection)

In a bittersweet preservation effort, the Brown Derby dome was spared from demolition, only to be wedged into a strip mall on the site. (1986, Anne Laskey/ Marlene Laskey/Wilshire Boulevard Collection)

Pickfair

(1919 – 1989)
1143 SUMMIT DR., BEVERLY HILLS

Pickfair put Beverly Hills on the map as home to the stars. In 1919, Douglas Fairbanks, Sr. bought a hunting lodge and fourteen acres at the foot of Benedict Canyon. He had the lodge renovated and expanded into a mansion. He and "America's Sweetheart" Mary Pickford divorced their then-spouses, married each other, and moved into what soon became known as Pickfair.

Fairbanks and Pickford entertained constantly, hosting Hollywood stars, royalty, heads of state, and other notable figures from Babe Ruth to Albert Einstein. Many considered Pickfair as the second-most famous house in the U.S., next to the White House.

The home was renovated again in the 1930s, this time by renowned architect Wallace Neff. Mary kept the house after her divorce from Fairbanks in 1936. Pickford opened the home often for charity events, but it fell into disrepair over the years.

Pickford died in 1979. Los Angeles Lakers owner Jerry Buss bought Pickfair the following year and spent years renovating it. In 1988, he sold the home to businessman Meshulam Riklis and his wife, actress Pia Zadora. They demolished Pickfair the following year after deeming it "beyond repair," though they kept the gates and the pool.

An aerial view of Pickfair, which made Beverly Hills the place to live for Hollywood stars. Many considered it the second-most famous house in the U.S., next to the White House. (1926, Security Pacific National Bank Collection)

Douglas Fairbanks, Mary Pickford, and friends at home. (Undated, Security Pacific National Bank Collection)

Even though she didn't live at Pickfair full-time after divorcing Fairbanks, Pickford kept the house until her death and opened it for many charity events. Here, she serves tea to soldiers during World War II. (1943, no collection cited)

Pan Pacific Auditorium

(1935 – 1992)
7600 W. BEVERLY BLVD., FAIRFAX DISTRICT

The Pan Pacific Auditorium was L.A.'s premier recreational venue for decades. Designed by Walter Wurdeman and Welton Becket, the 1935 building was also one of the country's finest examples of Streamline Moderne architecture. Its green-and-white façade spanned more than 200 feet and featured curved, fin-like pylons above the entrance.

The Pan Pacific hosted shows of every stripe—home, garden, auto, boat, horse, trailer, hi-fi, do-it-yourself, and sportsman, to name just a few. It hosted circuses, sporting events, ice skating, tapings of *Queen for a Day*, and appearances by everyone from Eisenhower to Elvis.

The auditorium couldn't compete with progress, however. It closed in 1972, a year after the Los Angeles Convention Center opened. As plans for the building came and went, it stood vacant, vandalized, and deteriorating for seventeen years.

A raging fire in May 1989 consumed the wooden structure, shooting flames 200 feet in the air. In a final indignity, the landmark's charred remains stood for another three years until the building's demolition in 1992.

The Pan Pacific Park Recreation Center now stands on the site, with a single pylon resembling those of its namesake. Replicas of the pylons also appear at the entrances of Disney MGM Studios and Disney California Adventure.

The main entrance of the Pan Pacific Auditorium at night. (1930s, Herman J. Schultheis Collection)

The valet staff of the Pan Pacific Auditorium. (Undated, Otto Rothschild/ Security Pacific National Bank Collection)

One of the first of many auto shows at the Pan Pacific, whose 110,000-square-foot interior accommodated a vast range of events. (1935, Art Streib/Security Pacific National Bank Collection)

Original caption dated April 13, 1954 reads, "James F. Jameson, student at Los Angeles Trade-Technical College, is the national bricklaying champ in an AFL contest at Pan Pacific Auditorium. A graduate of Franklin High School, he lives in Inglewood." (1954, D. Banks/Herald Examiner Collection)

Opposite: Original caption dated September 8, 1961 reads, "Actor Boris Karloff shows that he's a good skate, too, by perching the Meldrum Twins, Margaret (left) and Marlene, on his knees during intermission from their chores on ice." The photo was taken during the Ice Follies at the Pan Pacific. (1961, Herald Examiner Collection)

The Pan Pacific's largest crowd numbered 10,000 inside and 20,000 outside, who came to see General Dwight D. Eisenhower in October 1952, a month before he was elected president. "I Like Ike" fans waited outside for two hours until he spoke to them after a nationwide radio and TV address. (1952, Herald Examiner Collection)

Ebony Showcase Theatre Building

(1920s – 1998)

4720 W. WASHINGTON BLVD., MID-CITY

The Ebony Showcase Theatre was the first African American-owned theatre in Los Angeles. Nick and Edna Stewart founded the theatre in 1950 to provide African American actors a place to perform free from the stereotypical roles of the time.

An accomplished actor, Nick Stewart was best known for his portrayal of Lightnin' in the TV show *Amos and Andy*, and for voicing Br'er Bear in Disney's *Song of the South*. He used his earnings from these roles to support the theatre. After starting in a converted garage and moving a few times, in 1965 the Ebony Showcase moved into a 1920s building that had previously housed the Rimpau and Metro Theatres.

John Amos, Isabel Sanford, and Nichelle Nichols were just a few of the actors who came out of the Ebony Showcase. The Ebony also ran a children's theatre and an after-school "latchkey" program for kids who would otherwise be home alone.

In the 1990s, the Community Redevelopment Agency of Los Angeles seized the Ebony Showcase Theatre building by eminent domain. Despite assurances from the agency and Councilmember Nate Holden that the theatre would be saved, the building was demolished in September 1998. It was replaced by a performing arts center named for Holden and operated by the Ebony Repertory Theatre (no relation).

Original caption dated October 16, 1981 reads, "Nick and Edna Stewart have done a lot to change black stereotypes in theater with their plays since the days when Nick had an act as a comedian." (1981, Paul Chinn/Herald Examiner Collection)

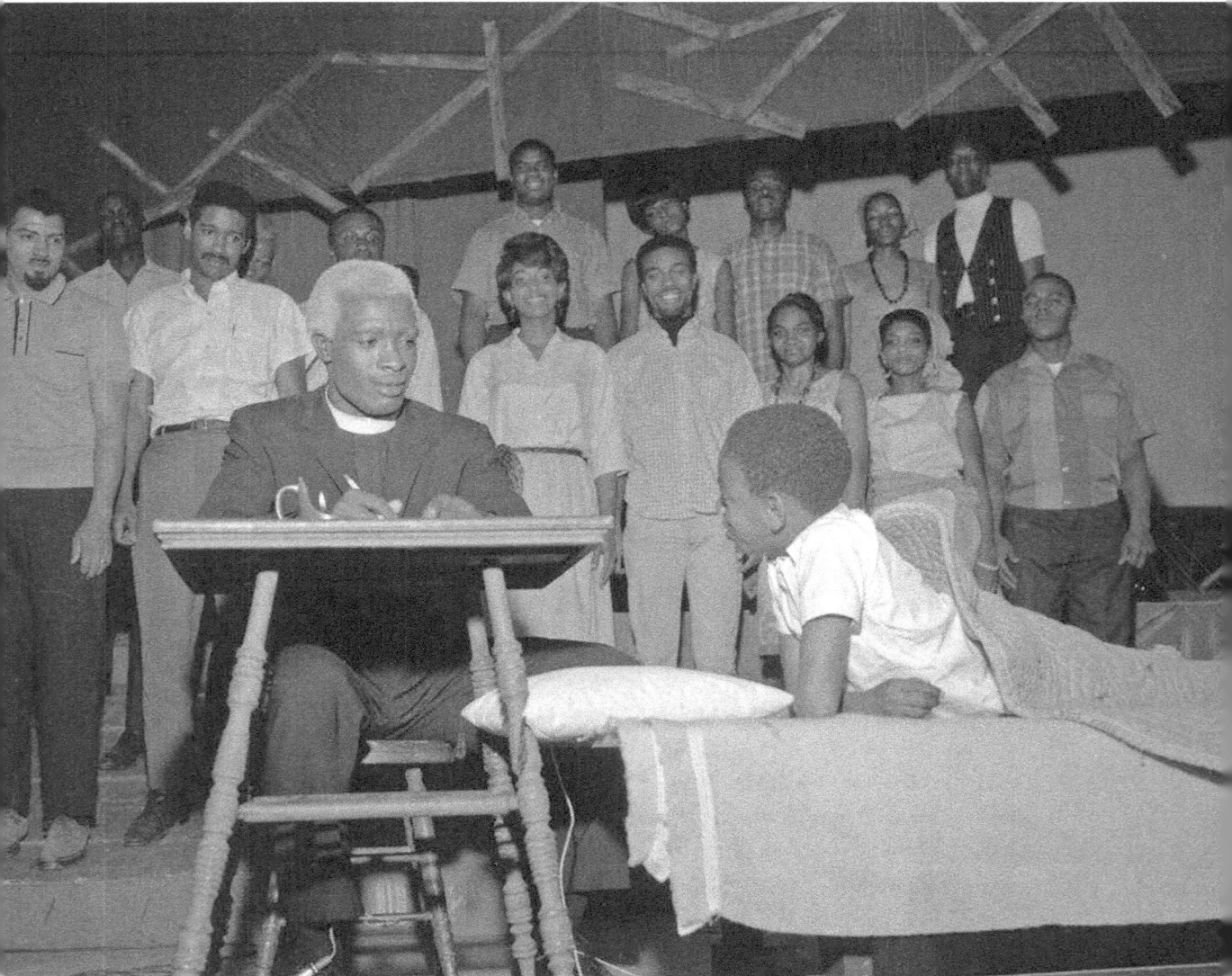

Actor Joseph Washington (seated) performs in *Lost in Stars* at the Ebony Showcase Theatre. (Circa 1967, Rolland J. Curtis Collection of Negatives and Photographs)

The Stewarts receive a commendation from then-City Councilmembers Tom Bradley and Billy Mills in 1966. Pictured are (from left) Unknown, Nick Stewart, Rod Serling, Unknown, Jayne Meadows, Bradley, Edna Stewart, Mills, and Steve Allen. (1966, Rolland J. Curtis Collection of Negatives and Photographs)

Woodland Hills Library

(1962 – 2001)

22200 Ventura Blvd., Woodland Hills

The 1962 Woodland Hills branch of the Los Angeles Public Library was one of hundreds of buildings constructed to serve new communities in the postwar San Fernando Valley. Architects Ralph Bowerman and Charles Hobson designed the brick-and-stucco building with dramatic curving eaves and a parabolic roof that seemed to float over the building. Walls of glass flooded the interior with light and brought the outdoors in.

After serving the neighborhood for decades, the

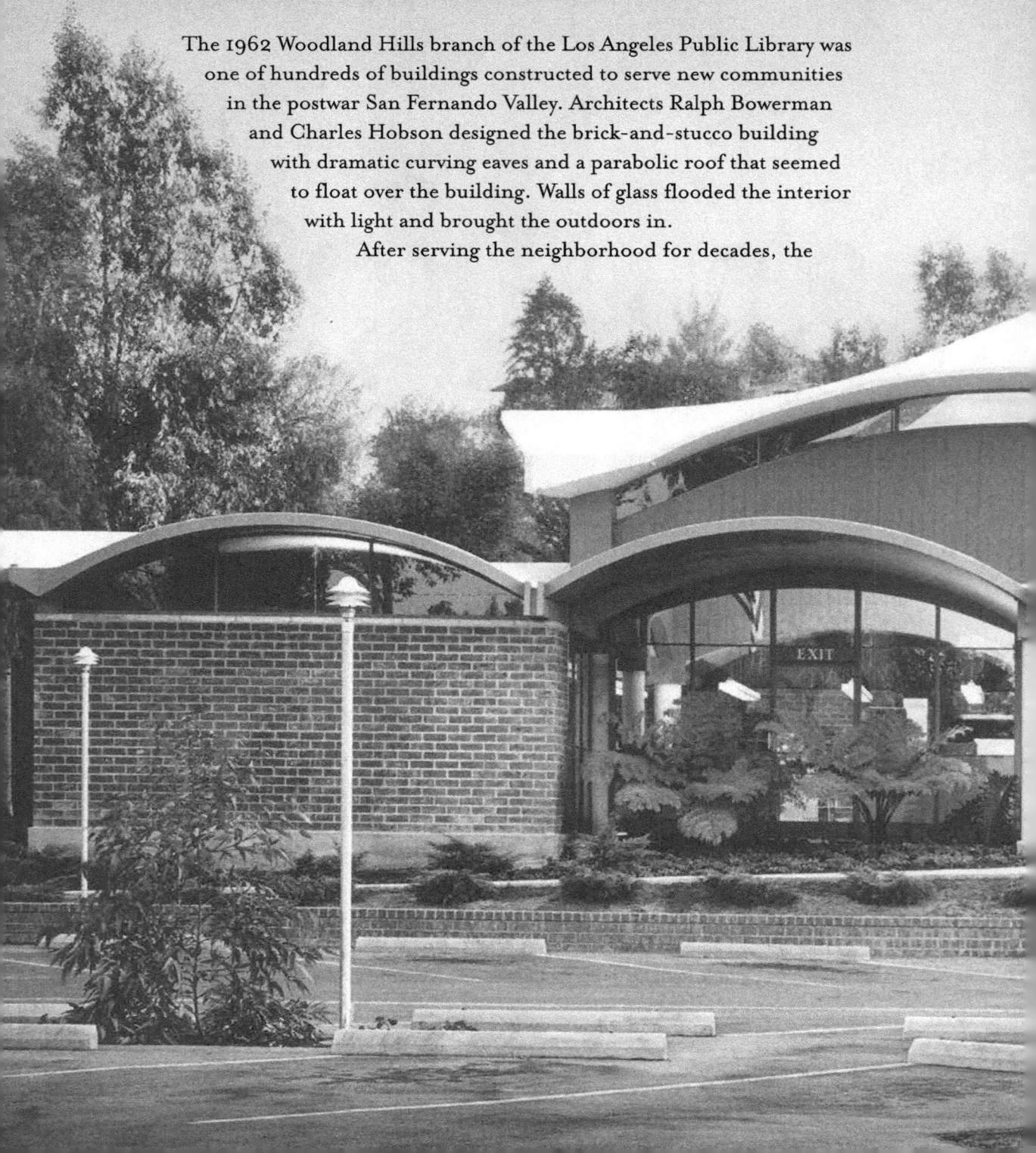

library had outgrown the building by the late 1990s. A library bond measure approved by voters in 1998 called for a dozen Valley branches to be demolished, renovated, or expanded—including this one.

The debate over the building's fate ultimately came down to a choice between this branch and another one in Canoga Park, designed by the same architects in 1959. The Woodland Hills branch was demolished in 2001 and replaced with a new building more than twice its size. The reuse of the Canoga Park branch as an early learning center earned a Los Angeles Conservancy Preservation Award in 2014.

The front façade of the Woodland Hills Library at night. (Circa 1962, Larry Frost/ Security Pacific National Bank Collection)

Overleaf: The same view during the day, all floating curves. (Circa 1962, Larry Frost/Security Pacific National Bank Collection)

In its first two weeks of operation, the Woodland Hills Library circulated 13,000 of its 18,000 books. Local residents and organizations contributed to an emergency supply. (Circa 1962, Security Pacific National Bank Collection)

Beverly Theatre

(1925 – 2005)

206 N. BEVERLY DR., BEVERLY HILLS

Opened in 1925, the Beverly Theatre was the first theatre built in the young town of Beverly Hills. It hosted vaudeville performances as well as films, and its opening night program included a filmed "tour" of nearby stars' homes.

Architect Lewis A. Smith designed the building for businessman Daniel Quinlan. The building contained the theatre and retail space, including Quinlan's real estate office. Smith blended Near and Far Eastern styles into an eclectic design capped by an onion dome, with an opulent interior to match. The theatre was renovated several times over the years, including a new façade that covered the original.

The theatre closed in 1977 and was adapted for retail use. It housed a Fiorucci boutique and, later, an Israeli bank that removed most of the remaining original features. Despite efforts to preserve the building, it was razed in 2005 for a luxury hotel complex.

The Beverly Theatre in 1937, screening the Fred MacMurray film, *Exclusive*. (1937, Security Pacific National Bank Collection)

The exotic Beverly Theatre screening *The Road to Romance* starring Ramon Novarro. It was part of the Quinlan Building, which also contained retail space, including owner Daniel Quinlan's real estate office. (1927, Security Pacific National Bank Collection)

The stage and proscenium of the Beverly Theatre. Carved elephants decorate the bottom of pillars on either side of the stage. (1940, Security Pacific National Bank Collection)

Ambassador Hotel

(1921 – 2005)

3400 Wilshire Blvd., Wilshire Center

The Ambassador Hotel was one of the most significant sites in L.A.'s history. Opened on New Year's Day 1921, the hotel was designed by Myron Hunt with later renovations by Paul Revere Williams.

The Ambassador housed the Cocoanut Grove, Los Angeles' premier night spot for decades; hosted six Academy Award ceremonies; and welcomed every U.S. president from Herbert Hoover to Richard Nixon. It also saw one of the country's most tragic events: the 1968 assassination of Senator Robert F. Kennedy, just moments after his victory in the California Democratic presidential primary.

As the city developed westward, the Ambassador fell into a slow decline. It closed in 1989. For the next decade, the building served as a filming location while the Los Angeles Unified School District (LAUSD) fought for control of the property. The twenty-four-acre site was a prime development target

in one of the densest and most underserved parts of the District. LAUSD finally purchased the property in 2001.

The Los Angeles Conservancy had fought to preserve the Ambassador since it closed, demonstrating how the iconic building could be adapted for new uses including schools and community services. Despite intensive advocacy, a range of proposals, and two rounds of litigation, LAUSD never seriously considered reusing the building.

The Ambassador Hotel was demolished between October 2005 and January 2006. Given the magnitude of the hotel's importance, its deep connections to generations of Angelenos, and its potential for reuse, the loss of the Ambassador Hotel is considered one of the deepest in the city's history.

Adding insult to injury, one of the schools that replaced the hotel mimics its iconic façade. *Los Angeles Times* architecture critic Christopher Hawthorne described the effect as "an odd mixture of progress and guilt."

The Ambassador Hotel fueled development along Wilshire Boulevard, which was a dirt road before it opened. This ghostly image of the main façade was taken from across Wilshire. (Circa 1937, Herman J. Schultheis Collection)

Opposite: The Ambassador hosted six Academy Award ceremonies, including the fifteenth in 1943. Pictured are Greer Garson and James Cagney, Outstanding Film Actress and Actor of 1942. (1943, Herald Examiner Collection)

Overleaf: An early view of the Ambassador Hotel, an icon of Los Angeles history and culture. The fight to preserve it was one of the toughest battles in the city's preservation movement. (Circa 1920s, Security Pacific National Bank Collection)

The world-famous Cocoanut Grove created lifelong memories for generations of Angelenos, famous and otherwise. Pictured is the Candlelight Ball on December 17, 1949. (1949, Herald Examiner Collection)

Edith Quong (left) and friends at the Cocoanut Grove in 1945, the first time Chinese Americans were allowed in the nightclub. (1945, Shades of L.A.: Chinese American Community)

Senator Robert F. Kennedy greets supporters in the Ambassador's Embassy Ballroom on June 5, 1968, after winning the California Democratic presidential primary election. Moments later, he was assassinated in the pantry behind the ballroom. He died the next day at Good Samaritan Hospital. (1968, Bob Shultz/Herald Examiner Collection)

After years of decline, the Ambassador Hotel closed in January 1989. Pictured is Eric Jacobson, who tried unsuccessfully to leave a tribute to Robert F. Kennedy including Kennedy's book, *To Seek a Newer World*. (1989, Mike Sergieff/Herald Examiner Collection)

Before the hotel's demolition, a public auction took place in September 2005 with items ranging from guest registers to furniture. (2005, Gary Leonard Collection)

Valley Music Theatre

(1964 – 2007)

20600 Ventura Blvd., Woodland Hills

The Valley Music Theatre was a community theatre for a growing postwar community full of entertainers. Designed by the firm of Hawkins and Lindsey, the futuristic dome was built by pouring concrete over a mound of dirt that was excavated after the concrete set. Inside, a theatre-in-the-round had nearly 3,000 removable seats for any kind of performance.

The theatre opened in July 1964 with *The Sound of Music*; the opening-night gala was studded with stars including Bob Hope, Danny Thomas, and the honorary mayor of Woodland Hills, Buster Keaton. Stars who took the stage over the years included the Doors, Woody Allen, Ginger Rogers, Charlton Heston, Vincent Price, Ike and Tina Turner, and many others.

After initial success, the theatre was beset with troubles and went bankrupt in 1966. Various attempts at reviving it didn't last long, and in the 1970s the building became an assembly hall for the Jehovah's Witnesses. The Woodland Hills Homeowners Association unsuccessfully nominated the building for Historic-Cultural Monument (local landmark) status. When the congregation outgrew the building, the church sold it in 2004. It was demolished in 2007, and the site sat vacant for years before luxury apartments were built in 2014.

"Star-stockholders" pose on an earth-mover at the groundbreaking ceremony for the Valley Music Theatre in December 1963. Art Linkletter sits behind the wheel, surrounded by Danny Thomas, Ed Begley, Janet Blair, Anne Jeffreys, Olive Sturges, Rose Marie, Ross Martin, Leon Ames, John Conte, John Raitt, Perry Botkin, and Marjorie Lord inside the wheel. Standing at the front is Ralph Bellamy, representing Actors Equity. (1963, Valley Times Collection)

Opening night at the Valley Music Theatre, July 1964. (1964, George Brich/Valley Times Collection)

Bob Hope with Master of Ceremonies Art Linkletter on opening night. (1964, Steve Young/Valley Times Collection)

The whole family got into the act at the Valley Music Theatre. In June 1965, the venue hosted the Summer A Go-Go, featuring the band Dino, Desi & Billy—meaning Dino Martin, son of Dean (right); Desi Arnaz, Jr. (center); and Billy Hinche. With them are Carol Keropian of Sherman Oaks (left) and Patti El Kouri of Encino. (1965, Valley Times Collection)

The Valley Symphony rehearses for an in-the-round concert in February 1965, with musical director James Swift (standing) and comedian Steve Allen at the piano. (1965, Gordon Dean/Valley Times Collection)

Co-founder Nick Mayo (left) lights a candle on a cake commemorating the Valley Music Theatre's first birthday. Joining him are (from left) George Gugler, bakery superintendent of Ralphs Industries, who provided the cake; Los Angeles County Supervisor Warren M. Dorn; actress Janet Blair (Mayo's wife); and City Councilmember Tom Shepard. (1965, Jeff Goldwater/Valley Times Collection)

Atomic Café Building

(1915 – 2015)
422 E. First St., Little Tokyo

Dating from 1915, this brick building at the corner of First and Alameda
Streets in Little Tokyo was the second location of the Atomic Café, a diner
opened by Minoru Matoba and his wife Ito in 1946. The café moved
here in 1961. Minoru's daughter Nancy helped run the business when he
became ill. A former singer with the band Hiroshima, Nancy brought a
punk vibe to the café.

In the seventies and eighties, the café became a popular hangout for
locals, artists, the occasional Yakuza, musicians like Sid Vicious and David
Byrne, and others who might be considered misfits. "It was a home for the
ones that didn't feel like they ever had a home," Nancy Sekizawa told KCET
in 2015.

The Atomic Café closed in 1989. Soon thereafter, former Atomic
patrons Sean Carrillo and Bibbe Hansen opened the Troy Café in the
building. They continued the site's musical tradition through the 1990s,
now with Chicano bands and Hansen's son, Beck. The site most recently
housed the restaurant Señor Fish before it was razed in 2015 for a Metro
station.

**The Atomic Café in 1982, windows filled with punk posters. Former patron Sean
Carrillo wrote in his blog *A Vanishing World,* "I once asked Mr. Matoba why he
chose the name 'Atomic' considering it was so soon after WW II and the bombings
of Hiroshima and Nagasaki. He replied, 'People will always remember the atomic
bomb. Maybe they will always remember the Atomic Café.'" (1982, William Reagh
Collection)**

Parker Center

(1955 – 2019)

150 N. LOS ANGELES ST., DOWNTOWN

The saga of the Los Angeles Police Department's (LAPD) former headquarters is a case study in the complexity of historic preservation.

The 1955 building was designed by Welton Becket & Associates and J. E. Stanton, with integrated landscaping by Ralph Cornell and site-specific art. When the Police Facilities Building opened, *Popular Mechanics* magazine called it "the most scientific building ever used by a law enforcement group." It was one of the first police buildings in the nation to centralize departments under one roof, and its design influenced that of police facilities nationwide.

As Chief of Police from 1950 to 1966, William H. Parker modernized the police force and reduced corruption. He also used aggressive, militarized police tactics to suppress crime, particularly against non-white residents. The building was renamed for Parker after his death in 1966, strengthening its symbolism and making it a hub for protests against police brutality.

Parker Center stood largely vacant after the LAPD moved to its new headquarters in 2009. The Los Angeles Conservancy advocated, to no avail, for its reuse as an important reminder of our complex past. In addition to what many consider a flawed and politicized process for determining its fate, the building's difficult history made it a painful reminder for many—not just the communities who suffered under Parker's tenure. Residents of adjacent Little Tokyo ultimately opposed its preservation, since Parker Center had itself replaced several of the most vibrant blocks in the neighborhood.

The building was demolished in 2019, slated for replacement with a City office tower. Its legacy may lie in deepening the conversation around what we preserve, why, and for whom.

The Police Facilities Building (later renamed after Chief William H. Parker) soon after its completion. (1955, Jack B. Kemmerer/Security Pacific National Bank Collection)

150 — POLICE DEPARTMENT — CITY OF LOS ANGELES

PARKER CENTER

Parker Center featured integrated landscaping and art, including a mosaic mural by Joseph Young depicting Los Angeles landmarks. (1955, Ralph Morris Collection)

Opposite: **The sleek façade of Parker Center, whose story exemplifies the challenges of preserving places with difficult histories. (2005, Brian Grogan/ Heritage Documentation Programs Collection/Historic American Landscapes Survey Collection)**

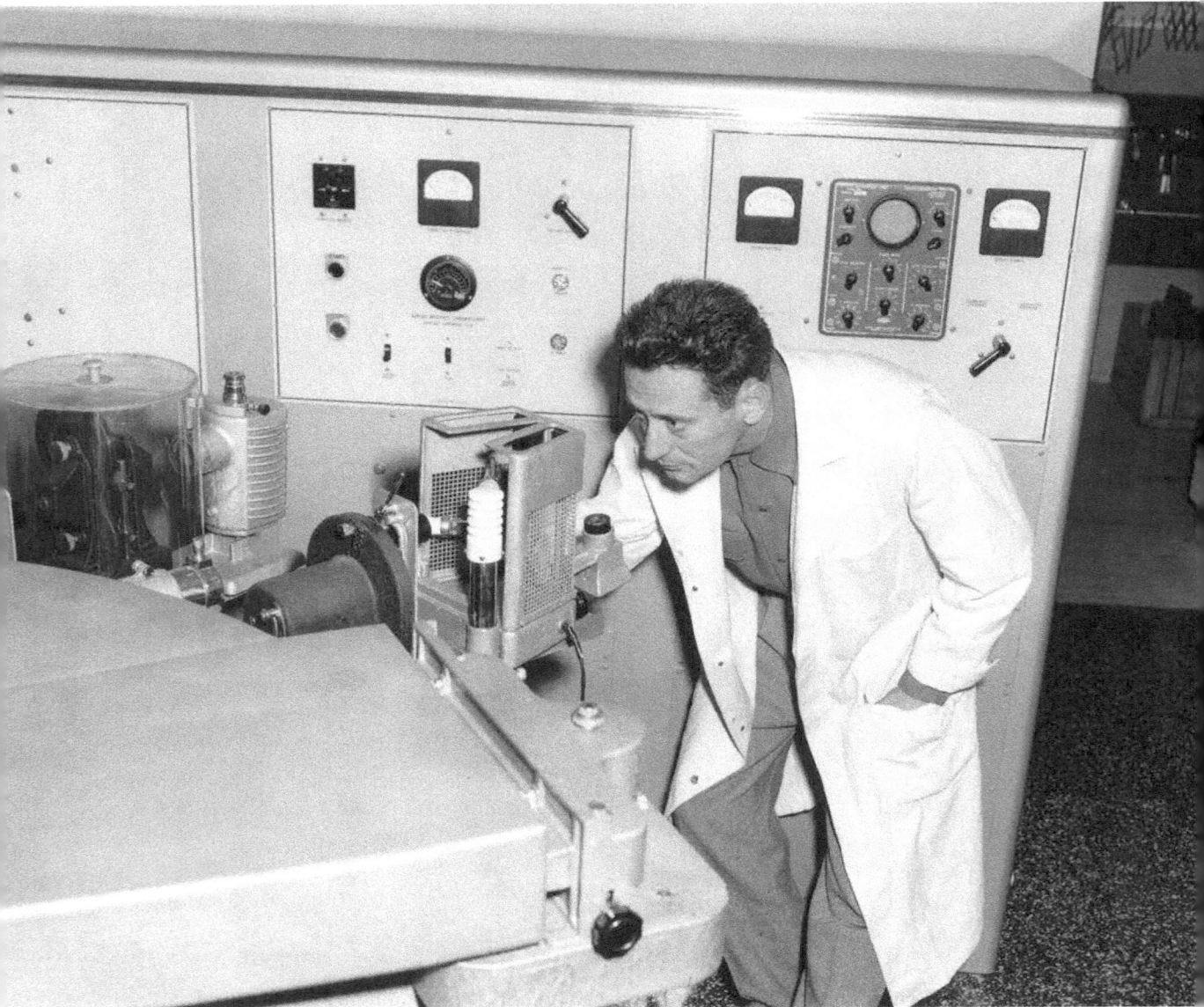

The building was hailed as a model of modern law enforcement; it contained highly advanced technology for the time, including this lab in the LAPD Scientific Investigation Unit. (Undated, Ralph Morris Collection)

Over time, Parker Center became a hub for protests against racial inequality and police brutality. Here, protesters surround the building after the acquittal of four police officers in the violent beating of Rodney King. (1992, Gary Leonard Collection)

LO

ALMOST
ST

Los Angeles Central Library

(1926)

630 W. FIFTH ST., DOWNTOWN

It's hard to imagine today, but we nearly lost one of L.A.'s most cherished landmarks, the Los Angeles Central Library. The 1926 building, designed by Bertram Goodhue and Carleton Winslow, is a monument to modernism with a nod to the past. The theme of "the light of learning" pervades the building, from the sunburst design of the rotunda dome to the handheld torch atop its mosaic pyramid.

Nonetheless, when it hit the forty-year mark in the mid-1960s, the library was considered outdated, too small, and functionally obsolete. Discussions of its demolition continued into the 1970s. As proposals came and went, growing resistance to the loss of this and other important landmarks led to the formation of the Los Angeles Conservancy in 1978.

After years of advocacy by the Conservancy and many others—and with the support of government, business, and community leaders— an agreement was reached in the early 1980s to expand the library while preserving the historic building. The firm of Hardy Holzman Pfeiffer Associates designed a massive addition that was distinctive yet complementary. Disasters including a 1986 arson fire and the 1987 Whittier Narrows earthquake delayed the project, but the expanded, revitalized Central Library reopened to the public in 1993.

An early view of the west side of the Central Library. (Undated, "Dick" Whittington/Security Pacific National Bank Collection)

THE·WORLD·IS·MY·BOOK

The ornate dome of the library's rotunda, designed by Julian C. Garnsey. The cast-bronze globe chandelier spans nine feet in diameter and weighs a ton (literally). This is an early view of the rotunda, before the addition of Dean Cornwell's murals. (Undated, Security Pacific National Bank Collection)

Opposite: The world is her book. (Undated, Security Pacific National Bank Collection)

A man holds 50 books in front of the library's "check-out/receiving" counter, watched by women who might have been clerical employees. (Undated, Security Pacific National Bank Collection)

Opposite: Artists Dean Cornwell (holding sketch) and Gile Steele (atop ladder) work with a model on one of the murals for the library's rotunda. Cornwell painted a dozen murals for the building, which were completed in 1933. (Circa 1927, Security Pacific National Bank Collection)

After years of advocacy and negotiations to prevent the library's demolition, an arson fire on April 29, 1986 nearly did the trick. The fire destroyed around 400,000 works (a fifth of the library's holdings) and caused extensive water and smoke damage to the rest. The arsonist was never caught. (1986, Los Angeles Public Library Institutional Collection.)

The Central Library remains a beloved landmark to Angelenos, including Lan, pictured. (Circa 1996, Shades of L.A.: Vietnamese American Community)

Opposite: **In a creative funding strategy, developer Maguire Thomas Partners provided significant support for the library's rehab in exchange for the building's air rights (the buildable space above it). This transfer allowed the developer to exceed current height limits for two buildings across the street, Library Tower (now US Bank Tower, pictured) and the Southern California Gas Company. (1989, Paul Chinn/Herald Examiner Collection)**

Wiltern Theatre and Pellissier Building

(1931)

3780 WILSHIRE BLVD., WILSHIRE CENTER

Soaring above the prominent corner of Wilshire Boulevard and Western Avenue, the Wiltern Theatre and Pellissier Building have been described as a "dictionary of Art Deco style." Stiles O. Clements of Morgan, Walls, and Clements designed the building, sheathing it in blue-green terra cotta and making it seem taller than its 12 stories. The Wiltern's opulent interior was designed by G. Albert Lansburgh, who also designed the interiors of downtown's Palace and Orpheum Theatres. The theatre opened in 1931 as Warner Brothers' Western Theatre; throngs of fans lined Wilshire for a glimpse of stars including Clark Gable and Joan Crawford.

The theatre began a steady decline in the 1950s, and its owner sought to demolish it in 1979 despite the building's local and national landmark status. Working with the Citizens' Committee to Save the Wiltern, a young Los Angeles Conservancy raised awareness, negotiated with the City, explored alternative uses for the building, and held a massive public rally. Developer Wayne Ratkovich ultimately bought the building and renovated it with architect Brenda Levin. The Wiltern now thrives as a live entertainment venue.

The Wiltern Theatre and Pellissier Building. (1956, Security Pacific National Bank Collection)

Looking east down Wilshire Boulevard at Western, when the Wiltern was still the Warner Bros. Western Theatre. The dome of another landmark, Wilshire Boulevard Temple, appears on the left, with the tower of Bullock's Wilshire in the distant background. (1934, Security Pacific National Bank Collection)

The box office and entrance of the Wiltern Theatre, with exquisite Art Deco detail. In the background on the right is the 1927 McKinley Building, also designed by Morgan, Walls, and Clements and demolished in 1998. (Undated, Security Pacific National Bank Collection)

The spectacular auditorium of the Warner Bros. Western Theatre (now the Wiltern), designed by G. Albert Lansburgh. (1931, Security Pacific National Bank Collection)

The Wiltern announces its comeback to Los Angeles as the marquee is turned on after years of darkness. (1983, Anne Knudsen/Herald Examiner Collection)

Opposite: **Saved from the wrecking ball, the Wiltern undergoes major rehabilitation in 1984; here, painters work on the lobby ceiling. (1984, Mike Mullen/Herald Examiner Collection)**

Photo by J.A. Ramsey
Dingman Studio
L.A.

Lasky-DeMille Barn

(1901)

2100 N. HIGHLAND AVE. (ORIGINALLY 6284 SELMA AVE.), HOLLYWOOD

In this humble barn, the Hollywood film industry was born. In 1913, producer Jesse Lasky formed a production company in New York with Samuel Goldfish (later Goldwyn) and Cecil B. DeMille. DeMille came to Hollywood and rented a barn at the corner of Selma Avenue and Vine Street, where he filmed Hollywood's first feature-length motion picture, *The Squaw Man.*

The studio merged with Adolph Zukor's Famous Players and expanded, taking over the entire block. When the studio moved to Melrose Avenue in 1926, the barn went, too. Through a long series of mergers, the studio ultimately became Paramount Pictures in the mid-1930s. The Lasky-DeMille barn was an integral part of the Paramount backlot and became a state landmark in 1956.

In 1979, Paramount donated the barn to the Hollywood Chamber of Commerce, which moved it to a parking lot across the street from the Capitol Records Tower. As the structure languished in storage, suffering from exposure, neglect, and vandalism, Hollywood Heritage decided to find it a permanent home.

The Chamber and Paramount donated it to Hollywood Heritage in 1983, and the barn moved one last time to Highland Avenue across from the Hollywood Bowl. The building became the Hollywood Studio Museum in 1985 and, in 1999, the Hollywood Heritage Museum. Hollywood Heritage continues to oversee its preservation and maintenance, using the barn to celebrate the art form it helped create.

Co-director Oscar Apfel (center, with arms raised) films the first scene of *The Squaw Man* outside the barn, which stood in an orange and lemon grove at Selma and Vine. (1913, Security Pacific National Bank Collection)

Jesse Lasky at the barn on the Famous Players-Lasky Corporation lot, its original location. (Circa 1923, Eugene Hilchey/Security Pacific National Bank Collection)

Attending the barn's dedication as a state landmark in 1956 are (from left) Samuel Goldwyn, Jesse Lasky, Cecil B. DeMille, Adolph Zukor, Leo Carrillo, and Y. Frank Freeman. (1956, Herald Examiner Collection)

Preparing the Lasky-DeMille Barn for its move from the Paramount lot to the parking lot in the opposite photo. (1979, Roy Hankey Collection)

Opposite: **The barn stands in storage across from the Capitol Records Tower. It suffered years of exposure, neglect, and vandalism before being rescued by Hollywood Heritage. (1980, Roy Hankey Collection)**

Above and opposite: **The barn en route from the Paramount lot to storage. (1979, Roy Hankey Collection)**

Bob's Big Boy

(1949)
4211 W. Riverside Dr., Burbank

Located in the Toluca Lake neighborhood of Burbank, Bob's Big Boy is one of the iconic coffee shops that helped define postwar Los Angeles. Wayne McAllister designed the 1949 building in the Late Moderne style, which blended elements of the Streamline Moderne with freer forms, heralding the exuberance of fifties coffee-shop architecture. Its 35-foot neon sign made it a beacon for burgers and exemplified L.A.'s booming car culture.

The restaurant's owner sought to demolish Bob's in 1992 and redevelop the site. The Los Angeles Conservancy's Fifties Task Force (now Modern Committee) saved it from the wrecking ball, making a case for its significance long before the renaissance of Mid-Century Modernism. They successfully nominated the site for designation as a California State Point of Historical Interest. Today, Bob's Big Boy is as popular as ever, with its history as a selling point.

Valley teens enjoy car service at Bob's Big Boy in Burbank, saved from the wrecking ball by volunteers who believed in its importance long before the revival of Mid-Century Modernism. (1954, Valley Times Collection)

(Former) Cathedral of St. Vibiana

(1876)

214 S. Main St., Downtown

This Italian Baroque-style gem at the corner of Second and Main Streets was L.A.'s first cathedral. Today, it's one of the city's few remaining landmarks from the nineteenth century.

It was built in 1876 and designed by Ezra F. Kysor, one of Los Angeles' first practicing architects. As the city grew, John C. Austin enlarged the building in 1924, including a renovation of the Main Street façade.

In 1995, the Roman Catholic Archdiocese of Los Angeles announced plans to replace the cathedral with a new one. The Los Angeles Conservancy waged a preservation battle that spanned four years, entailed two lawsuits, and spurred a backlash against the organization for presumably obstructing downtown's revitalization.

At 7 a.m. on a Saturday morning in 1996, demolition began with no permit or environmental review. The Conservancy stopped it, but not before the very top of the cupola had been

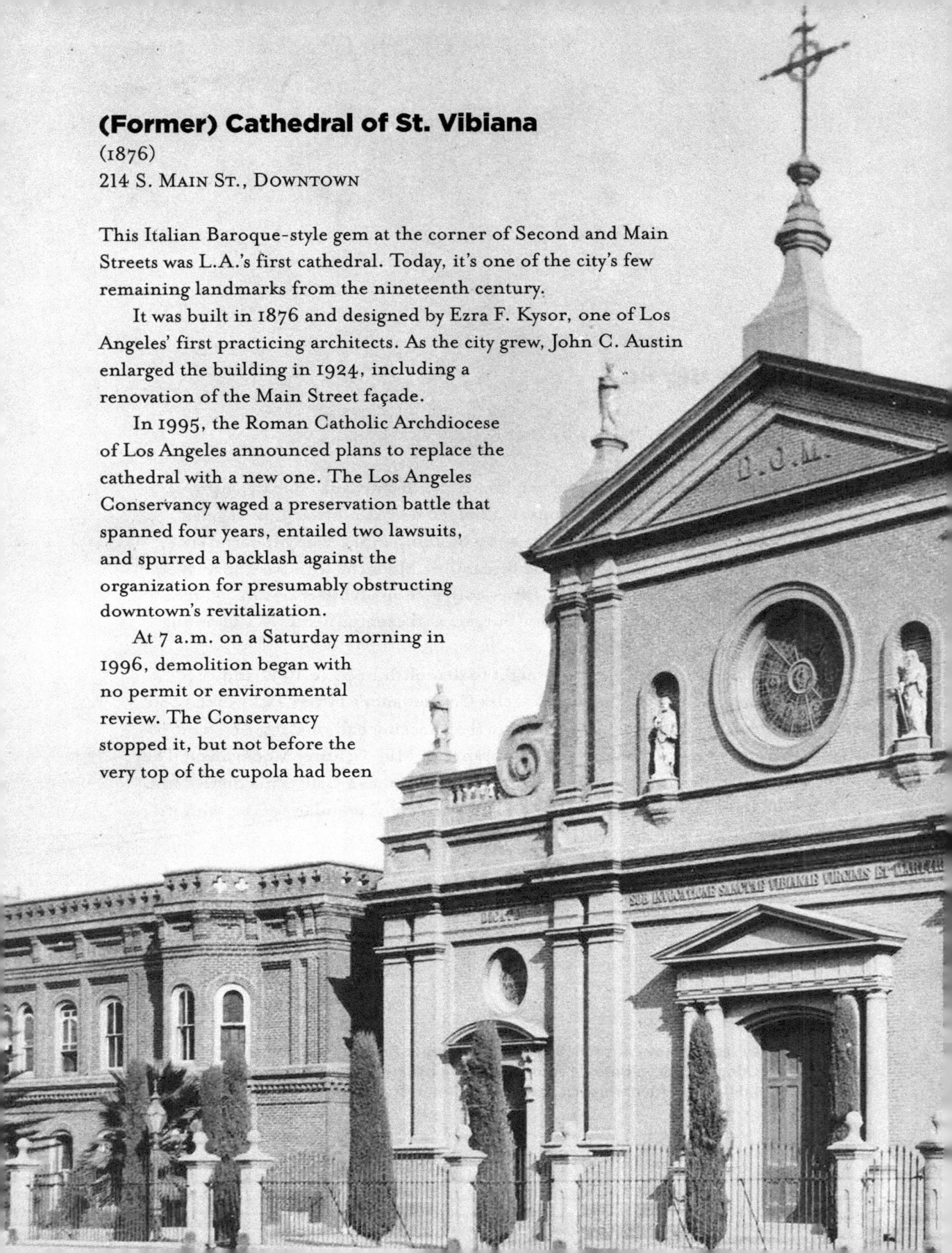

removed. After years of what would be one of the Conservancy's toughest battles, the organization found a buyer for the property and helped secure funding for its rehabilitation. Developer Tom Gilmore bought the decommissioned cathedral in 1999 and resurrected it as Vibiana, a popular event venue.

When it opened, the cathedral could fit one-tenth of the city's entire population. (1885, Security Pacific National Bank Collection)

Students at St. Vibiana's Parochial School prepare for polio vaccinations. (1955, Herald Examiner Collection)

Opposite: A wedding portrait of Ramon and Teresa (in a dress she made), who married at the Cathedral of St. Vibiana. (1932, Shades of L.A.: Mexican American Community)

Requiem mass at the cathedral for Robert F. Kennedy on June 9, 1968, after his assassination at the Ambassador Hotel. (1968, Herald Examiner Collection)

Opposite: **Members of the Catholic Daughters of America prepare for the twelfth annual Independence Day Mass at the cathedral. Pictured are "juniorettes" Cheryl Ann Rohland of Burbank and Toni De Mayo of North Hollywood (front); Linda von Gaertner, "state outstanding junior;" and Miss Dolores Lundmark of North Hollywood. (1965, Valley Times Collection)**

Once one of the few buildings in sight, St. Vibiana's Cathedral stands surrounded by skyscrapers. (1995, Gary Leonard Collection)

Opposite: Pope John Paul II stayed at the cathedral during his U.S. visit in 1987. Pictured are Ann Marie Capuzzi of the Greet the Pope Committee, and Sister Mario and Margaret Arnold of Women for Change in the Church, some of the protestors who demonstrated at the cathedral against the Pope's positions on issues such as homosexuality, abortion, and women in the clergy. (1987, Leo Jarzomb/Herald Examiner Collection)

Cinerama Dome

(1963)

6360 SUNSET BLVD., HOLLYWOOD

The world's first concrete geodesic dome was built in 1963 as a prototype for Cinerama, a new process that projected film from three synchronized projectors onto a long, curved screen. Welton Becket and Associates designed the Cinerama Dome based on Buckminster Fuller's patented technique, bolting together more than 300 pentagonal and hexagonal panels weighing as much as 3,200 pounds each.

The Cinerama Dome's unique shape, rising seventy feet above Sunset Boulevard, made it an instant landmark. Only a few other Cinerama theatres were ever built, making the Dome a rare example of a surviving, intact Cinerama theatre.

In 1998, the theatre's owners announced a redevelopment project that would engulf the Dome; destroy its plaza, box offices, and marquee; turn the lobby into a restaurant; remove the curved screen; and add stadium seating. A coalition including Hollywood Heritage, Friends of Cinerama, the Los Angeles Conservancy, and the Conservancy's Modern Committee persuaded the owners to preserve the Dome and develop around it. The Cinerama Dome became the centerpiece of ArcLight Cinemas.

The Cinerama Dome opened in 1963 with *It's a Mad, Mad, Mad, Mad World*. (1963, Security Pacific National Bank Collection)

With no development surrounding it, the Cinerama Dome was a highly visible landmark on Sunset Boulevard. (Circa 1965, Security Pacific National Bank Collection)

The Cinerama Dome's famous curved screen shows a demo film of a rollercoaster during the theatre's 25th anniversary on July 27, 1988. (1988, Chris Gulker/Herald Examiner Collection)

The Dome's distinctive profile appears in the foreground of this view looking east from the Hollywood Hills. (1987, Paul Chinn/Herald Examiner Collection)

Van de Kamp's Bakery

(1930)

2930 Fletcher Dr., Glassell Park

Yes, even bakeries can be historic. Especially ones designed
to resemble 16th-century Dutch farmhouses, like the
Van de Kamp's headquarters at the corner of Fletcher Drive
and San Fernando Road in Northeast Los Angeles. New York
architect J. Edward Hopkins
designed the building in

Early view of the Van de Kamp's headquarters,
the "Taj Mahal of all bakeries." (1931, Herald
Examiner Collection)

1930 to reflect the company's Dutch corporate image. Known as the "Taj Mahal of all bakeries," the building served as headquarters for the chain of bakeries and coffee shops whose trademark windmill buildings and neon signs pervaded mid-twentieth-century Los Angeles.

After the bakery closed in 1990, the building stood vacant for a decade before a big-box retailer made plans to take over the site. The grassroots Van de Kamp's Coalition rallied to save the landmark, which was beautifully rehabbed and currently serves as an educational facility.

This aerial view of the bakery shows the Van de Kamp's restaurant to the left (oval roof), complete with windmill. The restaurant was demolished; an El Pollo Loco now stands on the site. (Circa 1930s, Security Pacific National Bank Collection)

Opposite: The Van de Kamp's Bakery Cookie People, including Cherry Nut Shortbread Bar Wendy Becker, at a May 1983 celebration of the area's naming as Van de Kamp Square. (1983, Michael Haering/Herald Examiner Collection)

Golden Gate Theatre

(1927)

5176 WHITTIER BLVD., EAST LOS ANGELES

The Golden Gate Theatre is a treasure of East Los Angeles. Theatre architects William and Clifford Balch designed the building for developer Peter Snyder, known as the "Father of the East Side." Like many movie palaces, the 1927 building blended various styles to create a fantasy world—in this case, Spanish Churrigueresque with Art Deco flourishes including a scallop-shaped concession stand.

Designed for both legitimate theatre and movies, the theatre also hosted rock concerts in the 1960s, including bands in the legendary Eastside music scene. The Golden Gate is one of few remaining neighborhood movie palaces in Southern California, and it was the first building in East Los Angeles listed in the National Register of Historic Places.

The theatre stopped showing movies in the 1980s and was occupied by a church for another twenty years. The Vega Building, a historic retail structure surrounding the theatre, was demolished in 1992 after being damaged in the 1987 Whittier Narrows Earthquake.

After standing vacant, neglected, and vandalized for a decade, the Golden Gate was proposed for reuse as a retail drugstore in 2009. Local residents opposed the plan, lobbying for a cultural center. Ultimately, the drugstore plan was approved, and the Los Angeles Conservancy worked with the owner and a preservation architect to make sure the changes to the building were reversible and didn't obstruct the interior. As a result, the building can be adapted for other uses in the future, and drugstore patrons can enjoy some beautiful architecture as they shop.

The Golden Gate Theatre in 2011, a year before it reopened as a drugstore. Its entrance was modeled after that of the University of Salamanca in Spain. (2011, Tom Zimmerman/Heritage Documentation Programs Collection/Historic American Buildings Survey Collection)

The top of the Golden Gate Theatre peeks out from behind the historic Vega Building, which was demolished in 1992 following damage from the 1987 Whittier Narrows Earthquake. (1980, William Reagh Collection)

Despite years of neglect and vandalism, the Golden Gate Theatre building still has many of its original features, including the beautiful proscenium and balconies. (2011, Tom Zimmerman, Heritage Documentation Programs Collection/Historic American Buildings Survey Collection)

Closeup of the entrance of the Golden Gate Theatre, showing damage from neglect and vandalism. Buildings can survive extreme damage like this and still be rehabbed to continue serving the community. (2011, Tom Zimmerman/ Heritage Documentation Programs Collection/Historic American Buildings Survey Collection)

Lankershim Train Depot

(c. 1896)

11275 CHANDLER BLVD., NORTH HOLLYWOOD

Built around 1896, this train station at the corner of Lankershim and Chandler Boulevards is one of the San Fernando Valley's few nineteenth-century landmarks. It was one of the many stations that connected the Valley's agricultural industry to the ports on the coast. The nearby Bonner Fruit Company used the station to ship its goods, and the Pacific Electric Red Car line operated there from 1911 to 1952. When it stopped operating

The Lankershim Train Depot/Pacific Electric Railway Station appears in the upper-left corner of this view from the early 1920s. (Circa 1923, Security Pacific National Bank Collection)

as a train station, the wooden structure housed a building supply company. It then stood vacant for thirty years as its owner, the Metropolitan Transportation Authority (Metro), debated its fate. It was moved and placed in storage for years. Finally, after years of advocacy for its preservation, the building was moved back to its original location, rehabbed, and reopened in 2017 as a coffee shop.

The station in storage, waiting for Metro to determine its fate. (2000, Gerard Burkhart/Los Angeles Neighborhoods Collection)

Opposite: The station in the foreground, across from the North Hollywood post office. (Circa 1945, Valley Times Collection)

Century Plaza Hotel

(1966)

2025 Avenue of the Stars, Century City

The Century Plaza Hotel was the centerpiece of Century City, a "city within a city" master-planned by Welton Becket and Associates for the former backlot of 20th Century-Fox Studios. Minoru Yamasaki (who also designed New York's original World Trade Center) designed the elegant, crescent-shaped building for the Aluminum Company of America (ALCOA) – hence the aluminum façade.

The 1966 hotel was billed as "one million square feet of luxury." Over half a century, it hosted countless events for everyone from world leaders to celebrities to regular people. In 1969, the hotel hosted a presidential state dinner honoring the astronauts of the Apollo 11 Mission. Its popularity with U.S. presidents (particularly Ronald Reagan) made the Century Plaza a frequent site of political demonstrations.

In 2008, the hotel's owners announced plans to replace it with a mixed-use development. The Los Angeles Conservancy led the campaign to prevent its demolition, and the National Trust for Historic Preservation placed the building on its 2009 list of America's 11 Most Endangered Historic Places. With leadership from the City Councilmember for the district, and the mantra that preservation and development are not mutually exclusive, the Conservancy worked with the owner to make the historic hotel the centerpiece of the development. The project broke ground in late 2016.

Historic view of the Century Plaza Hotel, the centerpiece of Century City—and now, of a new mixed-use development. (Undated, Security Pacific National Bank Collection)

A doorman greets a guest at the Century Plaza Hotel. Can you guess which is which? (1969, Pacific National Bank Collection)

Opposite: Detail of the hotel's sweeping façade, which illustrates architect Minoru Yamasaki's fondness for ornamentation through materials and pattern. (1980, Carol Westwood/Los Angeles Photographers Collection/Carol Westwood Collection)

Jazz icon Ella Fitzgerald arrives at the hotel to accept the Whitney M. Young, Jr. Award from the Los Angeles Urban League, the first woman to be so honored. She's escorted by (from left) Dr. Madison Richardson, chairman of the L.A. Urban League, and John Mack, president. (1984, Herald Examiner Collection)

Opposite: One of the countless charity benefits at the Century Plaza Hotel, this one for the Crippled Children's Society Psychiatric Guidance Clinic. The event featured a Century of Fashions show; pictured is (from left) Mistress of Ceremonies, legendary costume designer Edith Head; an unnamed model in a gown designed for Ann-Margret; and Mrs. John J. Schneider, president of the Gold Diggers, the club organizing the event. (1966, Howard Ballew/Herald Examiner Collection)

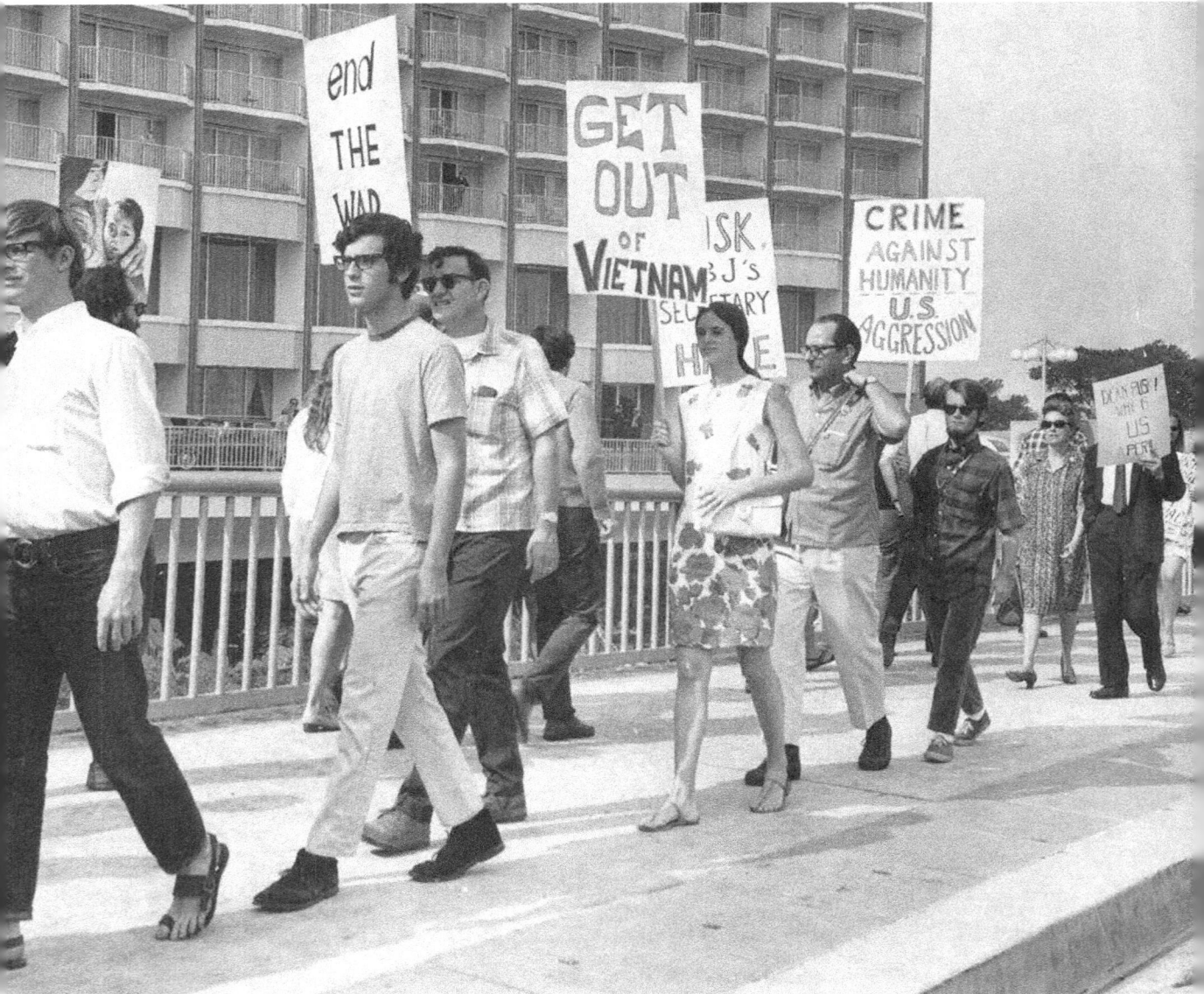

Vietnam War protestors demonstrate in front of the hotel in 1967, during a stay by President Lyndon B. Johnson. (1967, Herald Examiner Collection)

What's so hard about just saying no? First Lady Nancy Reagan delivers an anti-drug speech at the L.A. World Affairs Council luncheon at the Century Plaza. (1986, Chris Gulker/Herald Examiner Collection)

Terminal Island Canneries and Shipyards

(Early to Mid-Twentieth Century)
PORT OF LOS ANGELES, SAN PEDRO

How could a bunch of aging industrial buildings possibly be historic? If they tell powerful stories of key moments in our history.

The shipyards of Terminal Island were crucial to both World Wars and helped make Los Angeles a major world port. At the height of World War II, they employed about 90,000 people. They also saw the emergence of progressive labor policies to protect Southern California's growing African American population. Nearby, the tuna canneries on the island changed how America ate, making canned tuna a household staple. Terminal Island spawned both Star-Kist and Chicken of the Sea, among other brands. The industry was so essential to the area that a tuna appears on the official seal of Los Angeles County.

In 2011, the Port of Los Angeles announced a plan for the site that would severely limit the potential reuse of the historic shipyards and canneries—essentially poising them for demolition. The Los Angeles Conservancy led the effort to protect these overlooked landmarks, and the National Trust for Historic Preservation included Terminal Island on its 2012 list of America's 11 Most Endangered Historic Places. After years of advocacy, the Port adopted a master plan that paves the way for the preservation and reuse of these modest, yet important, elements of our cultural heritage.

Terminal Island's Fish Harbor, showing fishing boats docked in front of the Van Camp Seafood Company (home of Chicken of the Sea) and the French Sardine Company. (Circa 1938, Herman J. Schultheis Collection)

Esther (front row, center) and her co-workers take a break at the Southern California Fish Corporation on Terminal Island. (Circa 1947, Shades of L.A.: Mexican American Community)

Opposite: A ship under construction on Terminal Island. (Circa 1938, Herman J. Schultheis Collection)

Original caption dated January 7, 1942 reads (in part), "Continuing their all-out campaign to discourage careless talk about shipping and military operations in the Los Angeles-Long Beach harbor area, Naval authorities today began distributing thousands of posters driving home the vital message, 'Serve with Silence.' At the Terminal Island yard of the California Shipbuilding Company, Miss Jane Russell, motion picture actress, tacked up the first poster. The posters are brightly colored, with illustrations volunteered by Warner Brothers Art Department." (1942, Herald Examiner Collection)

**Nothing fishy going on here, just some private time on Terminal Island.
(Circa 1938, Herman J. Schultheis Collection)**

Sources

Bloomekatz, Ari B. "Developer wants to convert East L.A.'s Golden Gate Theater." *Los Angeles Times,* May 15, 2009.

Calisphere, University of California Libraries, calisphere.org

Carrillo, Sean. *A Vanishing World — Le blog de Sean Carrillo,* avanishingworld. wordpress.com

Castillo, Gloria. "Plans for Historic East LA Golden Gate Complex Growing." EGPNews.com, August 20, 2009.

Cinema Treasures website, cinematreasures.org

Colker, David. "On the trail of a lost architectural legacy." *Los Angeles Times,* November 13, 1999.

Guerrero, Al. "Memories of a Lost Boulevard: The Golden Gate Theater." *LA Eastside* blog, June 21, 2008. laeastside.com

Hawthorne, Christopher. "L.A. Unified's faulty vision for schools on Ambassador site." *Los Angeles Times,* July 18, 2010.

Head, Jeffrey. "Dodge House in West Hollywood: All that's left is the architect's genius and a cautionary tale." *Los Angeles Times,* July 16, 2011.

Hess, Alan. *Googie Redux: Ultramodern Roadside Architecture.* San Francisco: Chronicle Books, 2004.

Hines, Thomas. *Richard Neutra and the Search for Modern Architecture.* Oakland: University of California Press, 1994.

Hollywood Heritage website, hollywoodheritage.org

Kaplan, Sam Hall. *L.A. Lost and Found: An Architectural History of Los Angeles.* New York: Crown Trade Paperbacks, 1987.

Los Angeles Conservancy archives and website, laconservancy.org

Los Angeles Department of Building and Safety archives, ladbs.org

Los Angeles Public Library Photo Collection, photos.lapl.org

Los Angeles Times archives/ProQuest, lapl.org

McCoy, Esther and Robert Snyder. *Dodge House 1916.* 16mm film. Esther McCoy papers, Archives of American Art, Smithsonian Institution, 1965 (published on YouTube in 2011).

Moore, Andy. *Destruction (Neutra / Von Sternberg House Being Demolished).* Super-8 film, 1971 (published on YouTube in 2015). andystreasuretrove.com

Morgan, Susan. "Irving Gill's Dodge House: A legacy of beauty and invention." *Archives of American Art* blog, Smithsonian Institution, July 13, 2012.

Pacific Coast Architecture Database, pcad.lib.washington.edu

Rice, Christina, and Emma Roberts, eds. *Bunker Hill in the Rearview Mirror: The Rise, Fall, and Rise Again of an Urban Neighborhood.* Los Angeles: Photo Friends of the Los Angeles Public Library, 2015.

Roderick, Kevin, with J. Eric Lynxwiler. *Wilshire Boulevard: Grand Concourse of Los Angeles.* Santa Monica: Angel City Press, 2005.

"The Short, Happy Life of the Valley Music Theatre." *Peek in the Stacks* blog, Oviatt Library, California State University at Northridge, December 8, 2015.

Stewart, Valarie. Ebony Showcase Theatre website, ebonyshowcasetheatre.org

Turnbull, Martin. *About the Garden of Allah Hotel,* martinturnbull.com

The author made considerable effort to ensure accuracy and apologizes for any errors.

About the Author

A Photo Friends board member since 2010, Cindy Olnick is a messaging consultant specializing in historic places and preservation. She led communications for the Los Angeles Conservancy from 2004 to 2018, overseeing messaging, strategy, engagement, branding, marketing, digital outreach, and media relations. Cindy formed her own practice in 2018 to advance the field of preservation through strategic communications. In addition to her involvement in Photo Friends, she serves as Vice President of Public Awareness for Long Beach Heritage. A Georgia native, Cindy worked in communications in Boston before moving to Los Angeles in 2000, largely for its architecture. She loves Los Angeles and thinks historic places are magic.

Thank You

My deepest thanks to Tom Davies, my everything. Special thanks to Christina Rice and Amy Inouye for this great publication program, this wonderful opportunity, and their patience and indulgence. Many thanks to Carolyn Cole, Kathy Kobayashi, and everyone involved in the *Shades of L.A.* project, which allowed this book to show real people in historic places. Many thanks to Trudi Sandmeier, Alan Hess, Linda Dishman, everyone at the Los Angeles Conservancy, Kim Creighton and everyone who digitized and researched these images, Steve and Christy McAvoy, Richard Adkins, Mary Mallory, Naomi Hirahara, and the internet.

About the Photo Collection

The Los Angeles Public Library (LAPL) began collecting photographs sometime before World War II and had a collection of about 13,000 images by the late 1950s. In 1981, when Los Angeles celebrated its 200th birthday, Security Pacific National Bank gave its noted collection of historical photographs to the people of Los Angeles to be archived at the Central Library. Since then, LAPL has been fortunate to receive other major collections, making the Library a resource worldwide for visual images.

Notable collections include the "photo morgues" of the *Los Angeles Herald Examiner* and *Valley Times* newspapers, the Kelly-Holiday mid-century collection of aerial photographs, the Works Progress Administration/ Federal Writers Project collection, the Luther Ingersoll Portrait Collection, along with the landmark *Shades of L.A.*, which is an archive of images representing the contemporary and historic diversity of families in Los Angeles. Images were chosen from family albums and copied in a project sponsored by Photo Friends.

The Los Angeles Public Library Photo Collection also includes the works of individual photographers, including Ansel Adams, Herman Schultheis, William Reagh, Ralph Morris, Lucille Stewart, Gary Leonard, Stone Ishimaru, Carol Westwood, and Rolland Curtis.

Over 120,000 images from these collections have been digitized and are available to view through the LAPL website at **http://photos.lapl.org**.

About Photo Friends

Formed in 1990, Photo Friends is a nonprofit organization that supports the Los Angeles Public Library's Photograph Collection and History & Genealogy Department. Our goal is to improve access to the collections and promote them through programs, projects, exhibits, and books such as this one.

We are an enthusiastic group of photographers, writers, historians, business people, politicians, academics, and many others, all bonded by our passion for photography, history, and Los Angeles.

Since 1994, Photo Friends has presented a regular series called *The Photographer's Eye,* which spotlights local photographers and their work. In 2011, Photo Friends inaugurated *L.A. in Focus,* a lecture series that features images drawn primarily from the Photo Collection. We have presented programs on L.A. crime, the San Fernando Valley, Kelly-Holiday aerial photographs, and L.A.'s themed environments, among others.

With initial funding from the Ralph M. Parsons Foundation, Photo Friends sponsored the *L.A. Neighborhoods Project* by commissioning photographers to create a visual record of the neighborhoods of Los Angeles during the early part of the 21st century (all now part of the collection). To ensure the library's collection will continue to reflect such an important part of Los Angeles' history, a generous grant enabled Photo Friends to hire five contemporary photographers to document present-day industrial L.A. These images have become part of LAPL's permanent collection and are available through the library's photo database. Photo Friends also curates photography exhibits on display in the History Department.

Photo Friends is a membership organization. Please consider becoming a member and helping us in our work to preserve and promote L.A.'s rich photographic resource. All proceeds from the sale of this book go to support Photo Friends' programs.

photofriends.org

This catalog was published in conjunction with a photo exhibit at
Los Angeles Central Library's History & Genealogy Department,
curated by Cindy Olnick
On display in the History & Genealogy Department (LL4)
July 13, 2017 to January 14, 2018
Catalog updated in 2020

L.A. Landmarks: Lost and Almost Lost
By Cindy Olnick
Copyright © 2017, 2020 Photo Friends
of the Los Angeles Public Library
Images © Los Angeles Public Library Photo Collection

Published by:

PHOTO FRIENDS
of the LOS ANGELES PUBLIC LIBRARY
PUBLICATIONS

Photo Friends of the Los Angeles Public Library
c/o Future Studio
P.O. Box 292000
Los Angeles, CA 90029
www.photofriends.org

Designed by Amy Inouye, Future Studio Los Angeles

Special quantity discounts available when purchased in bulk by corporations,
organizations, or groups. Please contact Photo Friends at: **photofriendsla@gmail.com**

ISBN-13: 978-0-9978251-3-8

Printed in the United States